M000266036

THE CHIN...
GAME

The Best Kept Trade Secret of the East

CHIN-NING CHU

AMC PUBLISHING
BEAVERTON, OREGON © 1988

Published by AMC Publishing
Copyright © 1988 by Chin-ning Chu.

International Standard Book Number: 0-929638-19-0
Includes index.
1. International trade.
2. Negotiation in business -- China.
3. Business philosophy.
I. Title

Printed in the U.S.A.

First Edition: August 1988
10 9 8 7 6 5 4 3 2 1

Edited by Gayle Vrla
Cover Photographs by Jamie Bosworth

ACKNOWLEDGMENTS

For my Chinese friends who have made a significant contribution to the content of this book and wish to remain anonymous, I give grateful thanks. They hold a very special place in my heart.

I wish to thank Kurt Survance and Mike Germo for their diligent support. Without their assistance it would not have been possible to complete this book.

Furthermore, my deepest appreciation to the following friends who have supported, guided and encouraged me throughout the years.

Walter Beran, Vice Chairman, Ernst & Whinney

John Desmond, President, Flight Dynamics, Inc.

Kohel M. Haver, Attorney At Law

Jim Manning, Professor, International Marketing, Portland State University

Judy McKee, President, McKee Motivation

David Puryear, Dean, Graduate School of Management, Willamette University

DISCLAIMER

This book is designed to educate and entertain. It is sold with the understanding that the publisher and author are not rendering professional advice. The author and AMC Publishing assume no liability or responsibility to any person or entity with respect to any loss or damage caused or alleged to be caused directly or indirectly by any use of the information contained in this book.

The pin-yin system used in this book does not adhere to any particular consistent system. Rather, the combination of many different systems have been employed to express the Chinese words and names. In any given instance, the author has chosen the system that she considers to express the more popular versions of Chinese words that will best convey meaning to her Western readers.

ABOUT THE AUTHOR

Chin-ning Chu, President of Asian Marketing Consultants, Inc., is an international lecturer, writer, and consultant. Ms. Chu was born in China and completed her college education in Taiwan. In 1966, when Ms. Chu was 19 years old, she was entrusted with the marketing responsibilities of a government-owned pharmaceutical company and the medical products of two other European firms. Thus began her career in international marketing.

Ms. Chu's training in philosophy and psychology has provided her with a powerful tool with which to examine complicated Chinese philosophical, sociological, and historical effects on the workings of the Chinese mind.

Although she was a student of Catholicism from a very early age, she later expanded her horizons to include traditional Chinese philosophies, studying the philosophies of Lao Tzu, Zhung Tzu, Chu Tzu, Confucius, Chinese Taoism, and Buddhism. Throughout her life, Ms. Chu has studied Chinese history and its relevance to the behaviors that are prevalent today in the Chinese business world. In the early 1980s, she traveled to India, a land of ancient philosophers who created the roots of Chinese and Japanese Buddhism.

The knowledge Ms. Chu has gained in international trading and marketing development has come primarily from direct working experience. She has worked as a bridge between Eastern and Western businesses, in a wide range of fields -- including electronic systems, agriculture (machinery, livestock and seed products), aviation, animal by-products, processed and frozen foods and transportation. She has also helped Western governments understand and develop trade relationships with the East.

Ms. Chu's primary area of marketing interest lies in guiding American business professionals and governmental agencies to properly structure business and political practices with Asian countries based on the intricacies and interrelationships of the differing cultural and business styles.

PREFACE

Trade with the Japanese and Chinese is a subject covered by many books. These books reflect extensive research and accurately describe the actions of the Asian engaged in political and business affairs. The root of these actions, however, is so deeply buried that the underlying causes are difficult, perhaps impossible, for the foreign eye to detect and define.

Learning about the Asian's demeanor without understanding his motivation does not help you in negotiating with your Asian trading partner to your benefit. It is essential to penetrate to the origin of their behavior. American businesspersons cannot benefit from being aware of only the Asian's surface behavior and actions. These elements do not tell the whole story.

This book reveals the hidden secrets of business practices in the East. Secret strategic maneuvers have been a part of the Asian's life for thousands of years. They are an integral part of the Asian environment. They are practiced daily and have become so fine-tuned as to be almost impossible to recognize by a Westerner. Complicated strategies are woven about the unsuspecting American politician or businessman.

Americans have paid dearly for their lack of knowledge in dealing with Asians. They have often been the object of complex battle strategies. They cannot win if they do not know the rules of the mind game they are playing. Simply examining the symptoms without gaining insight into the cause is not enough. Without understanding the Asian businessman's hidden strategies, as well as his behavior and actions, it will be impossible to analyze present intentions and to predict the direction of future negotiations.

Uncle Sam has dumped millions of dollars of U.S. aid into Eastern countries, never suspecting he's been the victim of hidden battle strategies used to benefit the Asians. The Asians do not use these battle strategies maliciously, but rather as a function of their environment. Life is a grand game and they love to win through the art of maneuvering.

The results you will gain from reading this book are the ability to identify these strategies when they are used by your Asian trading partners, and a thorough understanding of methods to be employed in negotiations as counter-measures and counter- strategies. You will be given a rare glimpse of the inner workings of the Asian culture, and treated to unique insights about Asians not explored as intimately in any other English text.

CONTENTS

CHAPTER 7 THICK FACE - BLACK HEART: THE ANCIENT CHINESE SUCCESS SECRET 141

CHAPTER 8 36 STRATEGIES 155

CHAPTER 9 THE WISDOM OF THE CHINESE   203

1 THE HURDLES

The Frenchman's Story

On a Spring morning in 1986, a French madman was arrested by the police in Tienanmen Square in central Beijing. He had been screaming wildly and making obscene gestures at passers-by. The Chinese authorities subdued him and immediately put him on a plane for France. Upon his arrival in Paris, he was committed to a mental institution.

The man's name was Andre Pierre. He had arrived in China some nine months earlier as the representative of the French firm Petrofuture International. He had come to negotiate a $500 million dollar contract to build a petrochemical refinery in a Chinese province. Less than twenty-four hours before his abrupt departure, he had been congratulating himself on a job well done.

Certainly the time it had taken to set up this deal had been difficult, uncomfortable, and very confusing for this Westerner alone in Beijing who had had to deal with the strange tactics of his Chinese negotiating partners. But, as the contract was signed, bearing a comfortable profit margin for Petrofuture, it seemed he would no longer have to endure the strange Asian ways and would soon be on his way home.

There was only one small cloud on the horizon. A man named Li, a high-ranking official in the Ministry of Foreign Trade and Economic Relations, had requested to see him that afternoon in his hotel room.

As he waited for the meeting, Pierre's mind worked over the last nine months and the early mistakes he and his company had made in dealing with the Chinese.

From the beginning, Pierre was puzzled to be the man requested by the Chinese to represent his company during the negotiations. Petrofuture had not been certain how to respond since such a request is most uncommon in the international marketplace; and particularly because Andre Pierre was not Petrofuture's top negotiator. But, as they had no desire to start the negotiations on the wrong note, they agreed to send Pierre.

As he left for Beijing, Pierre felt somewhat indebted to the Chinese for having chosen him. As he knew the Chinese were in desperate need of a petrochemical plant, he expected to be home within a month.

In retrospect, the first mistake, and by no means the last, was Petrofuture's decision to send Pierre alone. He would be dealing with teams of Chinese bureaucrats and technical experts. He was also poorly trained for his mission. Although the firm had hired China specialists to brief Pierre, these "experts" had only scholarly knowledge of China, not personal experience. They warned him the Chinese are tough negotiators, but gave no clue as to how to deal with them.

Upon his arrival, there was a round of welcoming banquets which left Pierre tired and confused over such an elaborate and large-scale welcome. Furthermore, after explaining his company's position to one set of negotiators, they would suddenly, inexplicably, disappear to be replaced by another team. More than once a team disappeared and, just as suddenly, reappeared. It seemed he would be explaining his company's position endlessly.

At each session he varied his words, his phrases, his arguments. He looked for the best way to make an impression on these unimpressionable people. Pierre's variations on the same theme and his minor self-contradictions were carefully noted by the Chinese. They were subtly thrown back or used to rattle him to put him in an inferior position and off his mental balance.

The plans for the petrochemical plant which had been carefully put together in Paris were slowly picked apart. The Chinese, eager to conserve foreign currency and to make better use of their factories, insisted on providing some of the parts for the project. The quality of these parts was questionable. Pierre insisted, over the repeated objections of the Chinese, that Petrofuture could not take responsibility for the result if such parts were used. His stubborn refusal to budge on this point cast a cloud over the negotiations.

Pierre at this time also realized his company's mistake in overestimating the role of the Chinese central government in Beijing. Pierre quickly saw that, although the petrochemical project had been initiated by central authorities in Beijing, all negotiations had to be repeated in the provincial capital.

The provincial officials used the supporting data provided by Pierre to buttress their demands to the China National Technical Import Corporation, the central agency in charge of negotiating such contracts.

The Frenchman began to feel like a cog in the great mysterious wheel of Chinese negotiations. He thought he could find an ally in the provincial officials in his struggle against the Beijing bureaucracy. Instead he discovered he was merely a sort of ping pong ball to be batted endlessly between them.

Pierre set the initial price too high. He had been told often about what pitiless negotiators the Chinese were so he thought it best to leave considerable room in which to maneuver. To his chagrin, he quickly learned that the Chinese were aware of the actual prices for such equipment and that they had been negotiating for the same plant with Japanese, Italian and German companies over the past two years. Petrofuture was sought out not so much for its high tech expertise but as a way to energize the fierce competition.

In order to stay in the race, he had to lower his price. Although the prices the other companies were asking were available to him, he chose to make a dramatic impression by dropping his price 15% in one single move.

Pierre began to develop a fierce hatred of the Chinese, including the people, the hotel, the food, and the deadening life he was forced to live in Beijing. At the end of the third month, the talks were suddenly broken off with no explanation whatsoever. He assumed a decision was imminent so he waited by his telephone for weeks. Finally, they informed him they were dropping their demand about Chinese-made parts. This meant that the negotiations had to start over from the beginning.

He went back to the province and restarted the talks. Those he met seemed to have forgotten everything that had been discussed before. The position the Frenchman held was increasingly uncomfortable but, like a roulette player whose losses keep mounting, it seemed to make sense to keep going. Yet, a French banker had warned Pierre, "In China you have to know when to stop or you'll lose everything, including your sanity."

Pierre was in his sixth month in China when he finally received some encouraging signals. Various intermediaries, all claiming connections to people in high office, began coming around.

Petrofuture had done business with Eastern-bloc countries, and had learned they might need to grease some palms, they were prepared to go as high as $25 million. Pierre settled on an intermediary named Wang. Wang was supposed to expedite the contract once a down payment of $5 million had been deposited in the bank account of a middleman in Hong Kong. Pierre signed the transfer order and Wang disappeared, never to return. Meanwhile,the Chinese negotiators returned to one of their prolonged periods of silence.

Eventually a meeting was scheduled. Pierre was face to face with the head of the CNTIC, the import agency. Pierre's exasperation at the progress of the negotiations caused him to give the Chinese official an ultimatum. To his surprise, rather than asking the usual questions, the official remained silent. They sat without a word for 45 minutes. Finally, he signed the documents Pierre had prepared. It was finally over. Back in his room, Pierre broke down and cried with joy.

On his final afternoon in China, as Pierre sat recollecting the difficult nine months, Mr. Li arrived for their meeting. He came to notify Pierre that although the agreement was signed by the CNTIC official, as it provided for certain tax breaks for Petrofuture, it was not approved by the Finance Ministry. Therefore, the talks would have to start over once again. The next morning he was found making obscene gestures in Tienanmen Square.

The Chinese were willing to overlook the incident and continue their discussions with Petrofuture. The company sent a new representative and a few months later the contract was signed.

The names have been changed and some license has been taken with the details to simplify narration, but the story of Andre Pierre is essentially true. It appeared in 1986 in an article entitled,"Tough Talkers from China," written by Philippe Simmonot for the South China Sea Morning Post, a Hong Kong newspaper.

This is a story that should touch the heart of every person who has negotiated with the Chinese. Although an extreme example, it demonstrates a pattern which can be recognized by any Westerner who has had to deal with the techniques used by Chinese negotiators.

Western business analysts tend to call this an example of "tough adversary negotiation" and "shrewd bargaining." In his book, Chinese Commercial Negotiating Style, Dr. Lucian Pye describes the Chinese as "too clever," as having "thin skins," and being "hypersensitive." Pierre's story is not so much an example of the Chinese being clever or such tough adversarial negotiators, but more a story that points to the foreigner's lack of understanding of Chinese negotiating style.

Since the re-opening of China, Americans have gone there tempted by the potential of huge consumer markets holding the promise of great financial gains. Often they return with less than they expected. Their lack of understanding of the philosophy underlying Asian business negotiations often causes their own negotiating strategies to be ineffective. In many ways, the American business person is ill-equipped to deal with the Asian businessman in the subtle game of trade.

In the East, negotiation is an ancient game with an elaborate set of rules and formalized strategies dating back two thousand years. Not only is the American businessman largely ignorant of the rules, often he is not even aware that there is a game going on. The following examples will explore some of the hurdles you will face in today's Chinese market.

Killing Us Softly With Friendship

Friendship. This word has taken on new meaning since the reopening of China's doors. Anyone who goes to China or engages in business or political negotiations with the Chinese immediately notices the word friendship is used over and over again. Conversely, friendship is rarely mentioned between friends in China, nor is it mentioned often at business or political functions. It is used primarily in situations where a real feeling of friendship is not present. In order to fill a silence in a meeting among strangers, something may be said about friendship.

In the Chinese culture, when an emotion is deeply felt, the cloak of words is often considered inappropriate. Even in the closest of human relationships, husband and wife or parent and child, the words, "I love you" are not spoken. It has been this way in China for five thousand years. Western powers invaded China barely a century ago. Now, after thirty years of self-imposed isolation from the West, China is going out of her way to broadcast the message of friendship. Why?

Westerners are led to believe that the first step of doing business with the Chinese is to be friends. They must spend time and money, give appropriate gifts, drink the right wine and eat the right food, not to mention participating in seemingly endless toasts of Gan Bei (bottoms up) in the name of eternal friendship.

What does the word friendship mean to the Chinese businessman when he is dealing with an American? The American is a person with a totally different conceptual frame of reference, a person with whom he often cannot even directly converse.

There are two considerations in the Chinese businessman's mind. First, the personal consideration: It is currently considered fashionable in China to have a friend in the West. In this context, the word friendship is used to express the desire for personal aggrandizement. The second consideration is professional: A successful and profitable venture with a foreign company is the highest possible achievement for a businessman in Chinese Communist society. The Chinese businessman expects his expostulations of friendship to be reciprocated by business concessions on the part of his Western friend. The Chinese are proud of their worldliness in dealings with Americans. They use the word "Tean-Zan" (child-like) to describe the friendly, ingenuous Westerner.

The Chinese view the marketplace as a battlefield. They are in it to win. The word friendship is used to create trust where often none is warranted.

To the Western mind, a friend is someone with whom you can work out difficulties, one who will support your cause and with whom you share a mutual ethic. A friend is one who will transact business fairly. This is not the case in the Chinese mind. The American believes that the next natural development among friends after letting down their guards is the granting of favorable terms to the party in need. Friendship means something different among the Chinese.

Here are a few examples of what friendship means to the Chinese:

> When you or a member of your family are sick, go to your doctor friend. He cannot charge. When faced with a legal problem, go to your lawyer friend. He will not charge. An attorney's friends are entitled to legal services for his lifetime, free of charge. If you need to go away for a year, leave your child with a family friend. They will not charge for room and board. In fact, your friend will pay all costs incurred in caring for your child. They will refuse money even if you offer it. Tradition prohibits accepting money from a friend for services.

If a friend visits your store, a discount price is expected. If the shop owner is a really good friend, he can only hope to sell goods to you, at best, for cost.
If you take a trip to Hong Kong, you are expected to take your friend's broken camera or watch to have it repaired so your friend can save a little money in repair bills over what would be incurred in America.
If you make a trip to an area where your friend has relatives, you are expected to serve as a no-charge delivery service for anything from messages to furniture.

Being a friend has a significant meaning to a Chinese. A famous Chinese movie star and her husband, a noted writer and director, purchased a hotel in Hollywood as an investment. So many of their friends and relatives from Taiwan, Hong Kong, and Singapore came to visit (staying, of course, in their hotel and eating at their restaurant for no charge), that they had to sell the hotel to avoid deep financial difficulties.

Such customs are not limited to the Chinese but are shared to a degree by Asians everywhere depending on their political, social, and personal environments. These customs and attitudes have been ingrained in the Chinese character over the course of many centuries.

On behalf of a large American corporation, I hosted a group of Chinese businessmen visiting the U.S. The corporation spared no expense as we traveled from city to city on a private jet, receiving the red carpet treatment at each stop. The Chinese endlessly toasted their undying friendship, but prior to departing, they asked me to contact a direct competitor to the host company for them after their departure from the United States.

Friendship is a tool used by the Chinese with other Chinese. Likewise, it is a very effective tool in dealing with Americans.

Arrogance and Timidity

Of Westerners who deal with them, the Chinese recognize two distinct types:

Lin Yu Tang, in his book <u>My Country and My People</u>, wrote the earliest, and perhaps best, description of the more offensive of the two, the China Expert. Details have changed a bit in the 50 years since his book was published but Lin's China Expert is still recognizable in the 1980's. He has been living perhaps in Hong Kong or Taiwan and is, he believes, well versed in Chinese culture, with an understanding of the Chinese methods of negotiation. He can use chopsticks and knows how to say "Ni how?" ("How are you?"). He reads the English-language dailies over his breakfast of ham and eggs and feels that, in doing so, he is staying close to the political situation in China.

He cannot pronounce words of three pin-yen(a group of sounds which make up a syllable), and considers himself fluent in the Chinese language. But to conduct his daily business, he depends on his English-speaking Chinese colleagues. He ordinarily surrounds himself with English-speaking people, Americans and Chinese, but when with visitors from the United States, he insists on giving incomprehensible instructions to the taxi driver and the hotel waitress in what he believes to be excellent Chinese. He is proud of himself for taking his American friends to a back alley in Hong Kong to bargain for a better price, unaware that he was cheated just the same.

He believes and revels in the flattery he receives from Chinese officials on formal occasions. Although he has no real knowledge or understanding of Chinese history or philosophy, he enjoys speaking of the Ming Dynasty, Lao Tzu or Confucius. He is proud of being considered a friend of the Chinese, but thanks his lucky stars that he was not born in China.

When he returns to the United States, he gives speeches and writes articles for newspapers and magazines. But after five years in Taiwan, seven years in Hong Kong, and three years in Beijing, he has no idea what it is like to be a Chinese or how the Chinese mind works. He spent most of his time in private clubs and on golf courses. The idea of eating hot soupy rice for breakfast still makes his stomach turn. The Chinese tolerate him and praise him to his face, but they far prefer the second type, the non-expert, any time.

It is not a flattering portrait that Lin paints, but it must be said that he did not apply it broadly and indiscriminately. He had words of praise for many Westerners, and an especially deep and abiding friendship for Pearl Buck, who he felt was a compassionate and understanding friend of the Chinese.

The second type, the timid American, does not offend the Chinese as does the expert. But he is generally so worried about not knowing the culture, customs, and the mysterious Chinese behavior that he cannot effectively function. He is afraid to speak his mind or ask questions for fear he will offend the Chinese. He acts the way he thinks the Chinese want him to. By doing this, he jeopardizes his bargaining position by appearing too eager to please. These actions, resulting from a concern not to appear the fool by being ignorant of Chinese ways, send a mixed message to the Chinese.

There is a third type, a better informed, better balanced individual whose approach falls somewhere between the first and second type. This breed is, unfortunately, rare.

The Uninformed Informing the Uninformed

In 206 B.C., China organized the world's first government bureaucracy. After two thousand years of existence, it has become woven into a cocoon of red tape that is difficult to penetrate, even by the Chinese. More often than not, dealing with China has been a game of the uninformed informing the uninformed. Some U.S.organizations, after years of exchanging friendship and technology and expending millions of dollars to gain favors, have found out they were dealing with the wrong ministries.

I was once invited to meet with some important Chinese officials who were, according to my American host, essential to the achievement of his organization's objectives. I listened as the American skillfully interviewed the Chinese again on their position. Afterwards, one of the Chinese officials told me, "We really have nothing to do with this. The authority belongs to another ministry. We are so embarrassed. Over the past eight years, almost everyone in our ministry has visited the United States at this organization's expense, and they have presented us with state-of-the-art factory equipment as a gift."

A Chinese businessman once told me, "China is like a mystery palace and Americans don't know where the door is. The Japanese don't spend any money entertaining us, they just sit and watch until they find the door and swiftly enter."

Who's the Boss?

Americans think in terms of "Who's the boss?" "Corner the boss and you will get your deal." In China, the highest ranking person is not always the boss. Seniority and personal connections carry more weight than titles. The Chinese call this structure "Ho-Tai." It means literally "back stage," and plays an important role in decision making.

If a person under the Director is senior in age and has a greater involvement in the government and party or if he has a strong Ho-Tai (perhaps his wife's uncle is a high ranking official in Beijing), he is often the true leader. His nominal superior would look to him for decisions. It is of primary importance for a Western businessman to identify and cultivate the real boss.

The official version of things is that this ambiguity between the nominal and the actual leadership does not exist, but the reality is quite different. The Thirteenth Congress, held in October 1987, stressed the importance of separating the state from enterprise, giving enterprise more authority. But changing China is like trying to turn over an elephant. The stated objectives may be worthwhile, but the execution is often unsatisfactory and ineffective.

Language Barriers

The barrier of language is, of course, the main source of communication problems between the East and West. In May of 1986, during a business trip to Hong Kong, I chanced to read a newspaper article with the headline, "China Investors Also to Blame." The article described an address by Burton Levin, the U.S. Consul-General in Hong Kong, at a luncheon given by the American Chamber of Commerce. He stated: "It's remarkable how simple truths sometimes seem to be overlooked, such as hiring bilingual agents who understand the difference of operating in a Chinese business environment, being patient, and the value of having a representative spend enough time in an area to develop a first-hand knowledge of the market and the personal ties so important to doing business in China."

Mr. Levin's views, as stated in his speech, show a clear understanding of problems facing U.S. companies today who wish to be successful in their trade relations with China. Levin said language is the number one problem facing most foreign investors in China. He said, "I am sure most of you have sensed that the skills of the interpreters assigned to you in China are wanting. Heed my warning, your interpreter is more likely to confuse than clarify the issue." He advised people in business to either master

Mandarin or hire someone with a thorough knowledge of Mandarin and English.

I have conducted interviews with numerous business people in the course of my consulting practice. I have interviewed American businessmen who have done business in Asia, as well as Chinese and Japanese officials. My findings have been quite interesting. Most U.S. business representatives do not consider it a necessity to learn the language of the country with which they are conducting business. Yet, when I ask the Asians they tell me they consider it very important to learn at least a little English and study American customs. They also feel it is important for their American counterparts to learn some of the native language and have a certain understanding of the history and culture.

China kept her borders closed for almost 30 years. The people who fought the revolution are now over 60 years old and hold all the power in the Chinese government. Although these people showed an initial resistance to learning English when China opened its doors to foreign trade, the China Daily newspaper recently reported that over ten Chinese ministers are currently taking English instruction. For an American to master at least some smalltalk in Mandarin would win him friends and respect in China, and it would give him that extra competitive edge.

In the United States, a businessman will polish his communication skills so as to maneuver and handle the subtleties of business with which he must deal daily. One billion Chinese make up an ocean of humanity and the

American business person who does not speak their native tongue will feel lost in islands of noncomprehension.

Your Company's Image in China

Accurate translation of materials from one language to another is vital. This is a major problem facing U.S. companies today. For instance, an improper translation of company literature into Chinese can give a company a poor image.

The translation of business cards is also critical. To the Chinese, a name is very important. It would be to the benefit of Western business executives and politicians if they carefully choose names to be used in China. They can be names which are pronounced similarly to their Western names but attention should be paid to the name's meaning.

The right words together can portray a desirable image. Some words, on the other hand, will create a negative picture for the Chinese. There was an instance of a U.S. diplomat whose name transliterated into a word which meant "stupid" in both Chinese and Japanese. This shows careless translation to say the least. The Chinese do not simply pick a name. They may take months combining words to create a name.

U.S. companies must verify whether a name was done correctly or literature translated precisely. Extreme care should be taken to ensure the quality of the work. Otherwise, they may never know how their company and personal images have been sabotaged by a sloppy translation.

I have seen a company's sales literature and business cards that were translated by different sources wherein each translator created a new name for the company to be used in China. The result was that all the Chinese promotional materials from the same company indicated mistakenly that there were four or more different companies selling the same products.

Conceptual Barrier

The barrier that is even more deadly and more difficult to overcome is the "barrier of concept." This one I have learned the hard way.

Years ago, I was negotiating a business arrangement with the Chinese for a client. All the negotiations were done in Chinese. The Chinese negotiators and I seemed to have a very clear understanding of the obligations and responsibilities on the part of both parties to the negotiations. However, in another meeting, one year later, we found that our actual agreement was much different than that to which we thought we had agreed. After rehashing the original agreement for a couple of hours, we discovered that, although we all speak the same language and had thought we understood each other very well, we had not. The words were the same but the pictures we each had in our minds about the agreement were quite different.

Due to client confidentiality I am unable to give a detailed description. But, let me give you a comparable example. I fly from Los Angeles to Chicago, from Chicago to New York, then to London. You and I know that all we have to do is have a valid passport, call our travel agent and everything will be handled. We don't even have to have a great deal of cash on hand as just about everything can go on a credit card.

The Chinese people in China, however, will have very different mental pictures about making similar travel arrangements. Besides the impossibility of getting any airplane tickets, whether domestic or international, with less then ten to fifteen days notice, a visa is required for a Chinese to visit London. The whole procedure of obtaining a visa to London or any other foreign country is an entire chapter all by itself. And then there are the official procedures necessary to obtain the foreign exchange for international traveling purposes.

Now I have learned to be very careful to not just have the understanding of the words but, more importantly, to ensure there is a meeting of minds.

Use Culture as a Weapon

The Chinese, Japanese and other Asians know foreigners are eager to learn their culture. They also know it is difficult for any foreigner to feel really comfortable with the little cultural knowledge they acquire. This is a natural weapon used by the Asians. They may hide behind their culture when things become uncomfortable, when they wish to manipulate a negotiation or disguise the use of intricate war strategies, making the foreigner believe culture is to blame for negotiating problems.

The Japanese in particular are masters of this practice. Some American companies, even with an apparent understanding of the Japanese culture, experience difficulty in penetrating the Japanese market because of complicated distribution systems. They ultimately lay the blame on cultural barriers. The Japanese are very aware of the important role culture plays in international trade. They are very willing to drop their cultural differences when selling goods in the United States and are very flexible in adapting to American ways. But when it comes to selling goods in Japan, they add as many cultural barriers as possible, at times making them incomprehensible to foreign traders.

It is important for the American businessman to understand which situations are the result of true cultural differences and which are just manipulation strategies.

Superstitions

Most Chinese are extremely superstitious in their daily lives and business practices. When faced with an important occasion, they seek auspicious signs. There are Chinese books detailing the optimum time for given events, such as: getting married, burying the dead, breaking ground for a new house, opening a new business or making a political move. A Taiwan newspaper told of a terribly ill man who refused to go the hospital because it was a bad time for him to go. The Chinese communist government has promoted the elimination of superstition but it still plays an important role in the Chinese thought process.

On a return trip to the Oregon coast, a group of visiting Chinese saw a deer cross the road. The leader of the group was very pleased to have seen the deer. He considered it a very good omen that his venture with the American company he was visiting would go well. The pronunciation of the word deer in Chinese is the same as the word prosperity. This may seem insignificant to the Westerner, but the Chinese expect the business venture to be difficult or smooth depending on the omen received.

Some Chinese believe that in July (which on the Taiwan Lunar calendar may fall in August) all the ghosts in Heaven and Hell come to Earth. They are released for this one month each year. There are usually no Chinese weddings in July and people hesitate to make important decisions or to conclude negotiations during this month.

The Chinese people also give special significance to color. In certain parts of China, a green hat is the mark of a cuckold. A delegation from Taiwan visited a Midwest farmer. The farmer was very hospitable and gave a green hat to the delegation's leader, placing it on his head. The leader was so offended he removed the hat and threw it on the floor. White and yellow are also offensive because they are the funeral colors. In Japan, China, and Korea red means happiness, joy and all good things.

An Allegation about Japanese Auto Makers

I spoke with a Japanese auto maker's general manager who was stationed in China about certain allegations made by the Chinese. The Chinese feel the Japanese sell their best cars to the United States, their second best to Europe, their next in line to the Middle East, and the bottom-of-the-line cars to China. The Chinese feel they have once again been taken advantage of by the Japanese.

The general manager said they were having continual misunderstandings in China. He explained that the United States, Europe, and the Middle East have equipment requirements for pollution control. The equipment placed on automobiles to meet pollution standards is fairly recent technology. The Chinese have no special pollution control requirements, therefore their cars are equipped with very straightforward engines. He said the Chinese have interpreted the lack of this more recent technology to mean that the cars they get are technologically outmoded.

Misunderstanding and miscommunication between Chinese businessmen and foreign suppliers is often a problem when dealing with the Chinese in international trade. Chinese officials sometimes lack an understanding and knowledge of international practices. They do not always understand all the rules, regulations and requirements. Of course, misunderstandings with Japan may be partially explained by the fundamental distrust the Chinese have for the Japanese. The Chinese have had some very unpleasant experiences with Japan during the past 200 years.

Lack of Understanding

A lack of knowledge of international trade practices has led to other misunderstandings. When the Chinese purchase equipment, they assume the purchase price covers all necessary components to properly run the equipment. Often, this is not the case and each component must be purchased separately. The Chinese just buy the machine and wonder why it won't work. The paperwork necessary in China to acquire foreign currency to make payments adds more difficulties. Once foreign currency is obtained, it is very difficult to go back and ask for more to buy components. They may come back later and insist the additional components be a gift to them because the equipment won't work otherwise.

2 THE VIEWS OF THE WEST

Historic Experiences with the West

In the eighteenth century, Voltaire saw the morality and organization of the Chinese empire as "the best the world has ever seen." Tales of China's wealth and size stimulated the greed and imagination of European empire builders. When Lord MacCartney arrived in China, the Emperor of China acknowledged King George III for his sincere loyalty and obedience in sending a tribute mission. The Emperor informed Lord MacCartney that he should convey to King George that China was self sufficient and did not have "the slightest need for your country's goods." China's superior attitude was not limited to fair-haired "barbarians." For thousands of years, the only people considered to be civilized, even within China, were located along the Yellow River, the incubator of the Chinese ancient civilization. This attitude still exists to a degree among the people of Northern China when they judge the people of the South. Today, the Chinese call foreigners Lao Wai which translates to "outsider." This is a term of denigration.

Contemporary Chinese attitudes toward foreigners have been shaped partially by the unfairness with which the Chinese have been treated in the past. During the last few centuries, the West has viewed China as a rich prize, ripe for the taking and large enough for everyone to have a piece.

China has traditionally been the "Sleeping Lion," an isolated country, cut off from interaction with the civilizations existing beyond its borders. This was a self-imposed isolation which existed for thousands of years. Minor trade occurred but no contact was established with other governments.

Nanjin Treaty

The Opium War ignited when the Emperor of China prohibited Britain from developing China into a market for the opium which was Britain's main export crop from their crown colony of India. From a small beginning, British imports of opium to China had increased to some 22,800 chests annually. Special commissioner Lin Zhe Xu was assigned to Canton in 1839. He forced the English to surrender their opium and burned it.

The Nanjin Treaty of 1842 settled the Opium War. China opened five of its ports for trading with British as points of concession. A 99-year lease of Hong Kong was added to the treaty. Western powers received legal jurisdiction over their nationals in China and China was made to pay an indemnity of $21,000,000 in damages to Britain.

British-French Troops

In 1856, 13 years after the Nanjin Treaty, Britain and France requested they be allowed to station ambassadors in Beijing. The Emperor of China reacted with outrage when he heard of the request. He shouted there had never been such a ridiculous suggestion since his ancestors had established the dynasty. Britain and France decided the only way to achieve their ends was by force. An excuse presented itself when a French Catholic priest, accused of robbery, was executed by local officials in Guangxi.

That same year, a British ship registered in Hong Kong and flying a British flag in Canton harbor was boarded by Chinese authorities. The Chinese were unfamiliar with the concept of a ship's registration and the sovereignty accorded it by Western maritime custom. Twelve Chinese seamen who served on the ship were arrested. The Chinese, unaware of the symbolism which the Westerner holds for his flag, offended the British when they discarded the flag of the United Kingdom by throwing it into the ocean. China never had a flag of its own prior to the 1900's.

Britain's Envoy Extraordinary, James Bruce, petitioned the Cantonese governor to issue an official apology and release his twelve imprisoned seamen. Governor Yei released the prisoners but ignored the Ambassador's request for an apology. Subsequently, a British battleship attacked Canton. The people of Canton could stand no more. They organized and burned the British commerce building, shouting, "Kill all the barbarians. Not one should be left." Britain and France united their troops the following year, 1857. They notified the Chinese governor that they had scheduled a negotiation session to be held in 10 days. Governor Yei, however, used the two specialities of the Chinese bureaucracy to handle this warning. The Chinese are masters of the twin abilities to push away (ignore) and delay. The date of the negotiation session arrived and passed. The combined English and French troops attacked Canton and arrested Governor Yei. The governor was sent to jail in India where he died in 1858.

Also in 1858, British and French troops sailed north and conquered Tienjin. The Tienjin Treaty was then signed. The 20-year-old Emperor was reluctant to sign the treaty. His Court advised him that the treaty was merely a piece of paper and, being just a piece of paper, did not have to be complied with. It could be used expeditiously, however, to rid them of the French and the British troops. "When the treaty is signed, the troops will leave Tienjin," they said. "Then, after they are gone, we will simply not fulfill our agreement. Later, we will tell the foreigners that those who are responsible for not fulfilling the treaty agreements will be severely punished."

28

In 1859, the troops sailed to Taigu (the seaport of Tienjin) to renew the treaty. The Emperor's representative warned the troops not to pass the port of Taigu. The troops were to reroute ten miles north to Beitan because Taigu had defense systems. The British and French thought little of Chinese defense systems and so ignored the warning. Therefore, they engaged in a battle with the Chinese and were later assisted by American ships (an uninvolved third party). China claimed victory by sinking four ships and damaging six others. The Chinese government did not understand international law and made no protest of the American action. China's Emperor celebrated victory, believing this was China's new beginning.

The Burning of the Summer Palace

In 1860, European troops returned to the port of Taigu and seized the city of Tienjin. The young Emperor ordered his general to attack and destroy the Europeans. However, the foreigners' superior forces again forced China into a treaty. But, this time British Envoy Extraordinary, James Bruce, asked to present the treaty document to the Emperor personally. For three thousand years, no one had seen the Emperor without kneeling and bowing. These arrogant "barbarians" now wanted to stand face to face with the Emperor and refuse to bow.

According to the Cambridge University Press, History of China, Volume 10, negotiations with the Chinese began on September 17, 1860. Among the Chinese negotiating team was the Emperor's brother, Prince Tsai-Yuan. This team was attacked by the foreigners because they suspected the Chinese of setting traps for them. Prince Tsai-Yuan believed the Chinese-speaking foreigner, Harry Parkes, was the cause of these problems and that the British-French troops would lose spirit if Parkes could be silenced. So the Chinese arrested him. He and 39 others (25 British and 13 French) were incarcerated and put in irons. The Emperor issued execution orders from Beijing. But a Chinese official helped Parkes and the rest of the British to escape ten days later. The Frenchmen were executed.

After the arrest of Parkes, the British-French troops attacked Beijing, forcing the Emperor to flee North. China surrendered and the British-French troops entered Beijing. Beijing had been conquered before, but this was the first time the city had fallen into the hands of the Europeans. Beijing's conquerors in the past were the Mongols and Manchurians - barbarians also; but they were at least Chinese barbarians, not the European "foreign devils."

The British-French took revenge for the men who had died in jail by burning the Emperor's summer palace, Yuan Min Yuan, located on the outskirts of Beijing. Prior to the burning, the soldiers also looted the palace of its priceless treasures and raped women in Beijing.

It had taken over three centuries to construct Yuan Min Yuan (during the Ching Dynasty). The Chinese watched mournfully for three days and nights as the beautiful summer palace burned. They recalled the Chinese people's great sacrifices during its construction. The

Emperor's younger brother, with mixed emotions of anger and fear, signed the Treaty of Beijing.

The Invasion of Foreign Powers

After the French and the British troops arrived in Beijing, the Russians saw an opportunity to benefit from the situation by taking advantage of the difficulty the Chinese had in understanding Europeans. The Russians went to the Chinese Court to convince them that Russia could help rid Beijing of the French and British. The Chinese responded by saying, "We don't trust the French and English. Why should we trust you Russians?"

Meanwhile, as the French and British never intended to occupy Beijing on a permanent basis, they prepared to leave. But they were delayed by difficulties in logistics which caused the Chinese to assume the Russians were in there stirring up trouble. Sometimes the Chinese are so "smart," they outsmart themselves. They believed the Russians had sided with the French and English in retaliation for the snub they received at the Chinese Court. Thinking they were in a dangerous position and worried that if they didn't pay off the Russians there would be more "trouble," the Chinese agreed to sign a treaty with Russia. In this treaty, China gave 980,000 square kilometers of Northeastern land to Russia, including the seaport, Vladivostok, which, still today, is Russia's only access to the Pacific.

In the Northwestern Chinese province of Xinjiang along the shared border with Russia, there were riots and rebellions among the Moslem minority from time to time during the late 1800's. As the Emperor's Beijing government was geographically far removed from this area, Russia saw these incidents as a perfect opportunity to take the advantage and sent troops to Xinjiang. Russia was hoping that the Chinese government might ignore this far away territory and Russia would, therefore, effectively advance her border hundreds of miles into China. To Russia's disappointment, the Chinese belatedly sent troops and reclaimed the province. The Russians were forced to give the area of occupation back, but insisted that the Chinese compensate them with money and land for Russia's effort in protecting the Chinese interest.

This is how the Chinese government ended up giving an additional 620,000 square kilometers in the Northwestern territory to Russia, including three lakes totaling 45,000 square kilometers. Along with incidental losses, the total territory lost to Russia was 1,620,000 square kilometers, an area equal to approximately three times the size of France or five times the size of Japan. Each time China lost territory to Russia, it was accomplished through the power of negotiation in the guise of friendship. No bullets were fired.

The Russian-Japanese war of 1904 was fought neither in Russia nor Japan but on Chinese soil. Chinese civilians were the victims of that war and only Chinese property was destroyed. China lost the territorial rights of Vietnam to France and of Korea to Japan. The total loss of land from the Chinese empire was 16 million square kilometers.

Following the Beijing Treaty, China was sliced into pieces by foreign powers. Major and minor powers of the world each claimed a piece for themselves. There were divisions of as many as eight to ten foreign territories in a single city.

Uprising of the Chinese People

The Boxer Rebellion in 1900 occurred in response to these depredations by foreign nations. In Western popular literature and movies it has been portrayed as a treacherous and bloodthirsty rampage by the heathen Chinese. In China it was and is still regarded as a patriotic attempt to throw off the yoke of foreign domination.

China was more a sub-colony of foreign powers than a sovereign nation from 1839, the beginning of the Opium War, until the end of World War II when the Japanese unconditionally surrendered.

On May 30, 1925, the killing of a Chinese worker in Shanghai at a textile factory by a Japanese merchant caused over three thousand students and workers to demonstrate. The demonstrators encountered an English patrol which opened fire, killing and injuring more than thirty people. Fifty more people were arrested. At Nanjin Road, the English fired upon a second group of demonstrators, killing four people and injuring ten. On the 3rd of June, over thirty thousand students struck in Beijing in protest of the violence in Shanghai. Factory workers and students in Shanghai struck on June 10th protesting the terrorist actions of the Englishmen. A demonstration was held in Canton on June 23rd and the Anglo-French forces shot and killed sixty more people. On June 25th, Chinese businesses, factories, and schools closed for the day to show their strong disapproval of the violence perpetrated on them by the Europeans.

China has been hurt and abused by foreigners throughout recent history. Shrewd bargaining, tough adversary negotiating, clever acting, and the use of friendship as a tool by the Chinese may be the subconscious application of techniques learned from the actions of the West over the past hundred years. The Chinese people are history-oriented. They live every moment with a consciousness of history, learning from the mirror of past events.

Distrust

There is a bitter residue remaining from China's encounters with foreigners. There were signs in Shanghai's British territory prior to World War II which read, "Chinamen and Dogs Not Permitted To Enter." These painful memories are still fresh in the Chinese mind.

Abuse at the hands of foreigners has injured the pride of the Chinese people. The Chinese experienced excessive cruelty by the Japanese during World War II, far beyond the magnitude experienced by Western prisoners of war. The Chinese recently protested the Japanese government's attempt to rewrite their history textbooks deleting all references to Japanese culpability in World War II - references such as "invading" China and the "Nanjin Massacre".

The Rape of Nanjin

On July 7, 1937, Japan launched an all-out war on China. On December 9th, Japan attacked what it believed to be the capital of the Republic of China, Nanjin. For four days and three nights in December, fighting raged around the city. On the night of the 12th, Nanjin fell into Japanese hands.

The capital of the Republic of China had been secretly transferred from Nanjin to Chongqing in Sichuan Province, located in the Southwestern interior, so the Japanese failed in their attempt to conquer the seat of Chinese government. But after the occupation of Nanjin, Japanese troops engaged in two months of continuous slaughter of Chinese civilians. From infants to elders, they were slaughtered, some were buried alive. Women from seven to seventy were the victims of multiple rapes. In total, the Japanese killed 350,000 people in Nanjin. The river surrounding the city literally ran red with human blood.

Since long before Marco Polo visited China during the Ming Dynasty, China has received foreign guests with politeness. But the events of this last century have created an understandable distrust of foreigners.

Asian Views of Americans

Interviews have been conducted with nearly 200 immigrants from Japan, Korea, China, Hong Kong, and Taiwan in the United States. Most of them feel they prefer doing business with Americans to doing business with each other. They feel that dealing with an American businessman is much less complicated. Asian business negotiations can be extremely exhausting and tiresome even to Asians!

Asians believe (whether correctly or not) that Americans are open, big-hearted, friendly, and trusting. American businessmen tend to trust other people more than do Asians. Americans are known to give generously to the needy and support worthwhile projects to lessen human suffering. They usually conduct business dealings at a relatively high level of integrity. Many Americans remain, despite the many set-backs of recent years, an idealistic people. The people of the East admire these qualities.

However, those qualities which the Chinese find endearing can become a liability for Americans in business and political dealings. Openness and trust can cause them to be vulnerable when negotiating with Chinese. It is relatively easy for Asians to pinpoint American weaknesses and use them to their full advantage.

Asians also find Americans to be sometimes too superficial. They often only look at the surface of problems while Asians dig deep. This superficial attitude makes dealing with Americans both easy and difficult.

Americans can be short-sighted. Their trusting nature can sometimes work against them. But the naivete of the American results, at times, from arrogance. The American may simply lack the interest or commitment necessary to learn the sources of his Asian business counterpart's actions and attitudes. Americans are often more interested in studying statistics of the gross national product than in studying culture or history.

Many American companies are notoriously impatient. They put a great deal of pressure on their representatives to achieve immediate results that will show up positively on the next quarterly report.

The Asian people feel these negative qualities impair the Americans' understanding of Asia and impede progress towards better trade and political relationships.

The American is certainly well received by the people of the East, but leaves himself vulnerable. The Chinese people call the Americans Tean-Zen, which means Innocent Children. They feel American history is simple, uncomplicated, short, and rather pleasant. It is a history of growth and relative peace. The American culture has not endured hardships like the ancient culture of the Chinese. The Chinese carry the burden of five thousand years of history of war, suffering, and the endless struggle for survival. Human life has been cheap throughout China's history, with a resulting loss of innocence and trust.

In today's international trade economy, the Western business person is wise to recognize the shadow cast by the past one hundred and fifty years of mistreatment that the Chinese have suffered. In consideration of their recent history, one can little wonder why the Chinese may feel they have the right to take advantage when the opportunity is presented.

3 HISTORICAL AND CULTURAL CONNECTIONS AMONG THE ASIAN PEOPLES

The Children of Yan Di and Huang Di

Before there were Japanese, before there were Koreans, there were the Chinese. The Chinese people believe they are the children of Yan Di and Huang Di. Chinese mythology describes Huang Di as the God of gods who gave up his divinity to abide on Earth and help mankind. Huang Di invented written characters and the compass. His wife, Leizhu, originated Sericulture (the raising of keeping of silkworms for the production of raw silk) and silk weaving techniques. In Chinese mythology, Yan Di is the Sun God. He teaches planting, agriculture and medicine. The intermarriage of the people of Huang Di and Yan Di created the Han people who lived around the Yellow River and gave birth to the Chinese race and civilization. Chinese written history begins in 2697 B.C., during the time of Huang Di.

During the Chin Dynasty, in 221 B.C., the Emperor of Chin united China and called himself Chin Shi Huang which means the First Emperor. Chin Shi Huang sought a method or medicine to create immortality. In his quest, he heard of an island east of China called Peng Lai, which is present-day Taiwan. It was believed this island possessed herbs which could confer immortality. In 219 B.C., Chin Shi Huang sent one of his medicinemen, Shufu, to find the island and bring back the magic herbs. Shufu asked the Emperor to give him thousands of virgin girls and boys for his voyage. He set out to sea but soon encountered a typhoon which drove him off course. He landed in what is present- day Japan. The young people he had with him married among themselves and with the natives of the island and begat the Japanese race. At least that is what the Chinese believe. The Japanese have a somewhat different view of their antecedents.

In 627 A.D., a Chinese monk, Xuan-Zhung, journeyed to India to acquire the holy scriptures. In 645 A.D., he returned to the capital, Changan. He brought with him the seeds of Chinese Buddhism. Japan, at the time of the Tang Dynasty (the golden era of China), sent scholars and monks to study Chinese culture, art, history and philosophy, as well as China's new-found religion. Through the visiting Japanese scholars and monks, the faith evolved into Japanese Zen-Buddhism .

Following the Shang Dynasty, at the beginning of the Zhou Dynasty, the Chinese Emperor declared Korea a Chinese territory and appointed Jizhu, a loyal subject of the Chinese Emperor, to govern it. The Emperor made Jizhu the Lord of Korea in 1121 B.C. Korea was officially under Jizhu's control when the Chinese people began to settle there.

Later, in 342 A.D., during the Jien Dynasty, China reconquered Korea. And, during the Tang Dynasty, from 644 A.D. through 668 A.D., China used its extensive military forces to again conquer Korea. Korea remained a Chinese territory until 1895, when it was lost to Japan who declared it an independent country. The Japanese later, however, occupied Korea as their colony.

History tells us the people of China, Japan and Korea are very closely connected. There are shared values through the agency of a similar culture and philosophy. Although the Chinese, Japanese and Korean cultures are similar in the broad strokes, there are important differences.

Geographic conditions had a great deal to do with shaping differences in the national characters of Japan, China, and Korea. Japan is surrounded by the sea, while China has a vast interior. The Japanese have developed what they call the island characteristic. The Japanese refer to themselves as "shi ma gu ni kon jo," which, translated literally, means Island Country Root Nature. This implies the characteristics which the Japanese honor, such as efficiency and eagerness to get things done. The Japanese are goal-oriented, objective people and gear themselves to fulfill their objectives. Thus, the Japanese have become an "organization" society, notable for working together to achieve consensus and extremely loyal to country and business affiliations. However, they tend not to be individualistic, except for their rare charismatic leaders.

Korea, although not an island, is a peninsula on the fringe of the vastness of China. Furthermore, the land was and is inhabited by a stubborn, resourceful people who have managed, against great odds and many invaders, to maintain a surprising degree of racial homogeneity. Korea developed along its own path and falls somewhere between China and Japan culturally. The Koreans are more efficient than the Chinese, but less energetic and productive than the Japanese.

Life is harder for the Japanese and Koreans because they are both surrounded by the sea, which limits their access to the natural resources that the peoples of China have in abundance. Through their more intensified struggle for survival, they have developed the national traits of greater eagerness, efficiency and aggressiveness. They tend to act quite a bit as if they "had something to prove." The Chinese have a much more relaxed, easier manner toward life and the world.

The Chinese have a different interpretation of bravery. They look to the long-range goal and feel that its attainment is more important than an immediate display of bravery. The Chinese often use retreat and escape as a strategy for future advance. Chinese troops may retreat from a superior force many times to regroup and attack again.

The Japanese and Koreans, on the other hand, are eager to die in battle and extremely brave on the battlefield. The Japanese are more inclined to be fanatics. If the situation seems to justify it, they will go to great lengths to achieve their goals.

The Main Currents of Chinese Philosophy and Religion

Philosophy and religion are very important in Asian society because they are more closely connected to each other and to everyday life than in the West. To gain a deeper understanding of the Chinese with whom you must deal in the world of business, you should make some effort to understand the principles from which their actions spring.

Yin and Yang

Portrayed on the Korean flag is the symbol of Yin and Yang: darkness and light. This concept dominates every aspect of Asian life. In Chinese philosophy everything in the world has a positive and negative side; a black and a white, a good and an evil, a dark and a light, a female and a male aspect. Yin and Yang balance the universe.

The oldest and most complete book of Chinese mythology is the Mountain Sea Scripture. It is a combination of works from the Hsia Dynasty (2205-1766 B.C.) and Zhou Dynasty (1122 to 770 B.C.), the Autumn-Spring Period (770-476 B.C.), the Warring States (476-221 B.C.), and the early Han Period (206 B.C.). The Mountain Sea Scripture contains several versions of creation.

Another version of creation is found in a collection of books called Huai-Nan-Zi. Both the Mountain Sea Scripture and the Huai-Nan-Zi relate the creation process as a combining of Yin and Yang forces; the female and male aspects of energy.

Asian society has no clearly defined division between religion and philosophy. Faith and philosophy are lived each day as a way of life. The teachings of Chinese sages are not generally regarded as the Revealed Word of God, but are guides to learn how to live in harmony with Heaven. The two most important philosophies in China are Lao Tzu's and Zhung Tzu's Taoism, and Confucianism.

The philosophy of the Tao preceded the Taoist religion. Lao Tzu and Zhung Tzu (circa 300 B.C.) did not start a religion. They merely taught the Higher Truth existing in the universe as they experienced it. Later, followers established Taoism as a religion and proclaimed Lao Tzu as their spiritual guide. They practiced superstitions and magic, and sought immortality. These were never part of Lao Tzu's teaching.

Buddhism, Zen, and Taoism

Throughout Western history, wars have been motivated by religion. From the Crusades to the Catholic-Protestant struggle in present-day Ireland, religious differences have led to war. The American continent was first settled by people seeking a place to practice their religious beliefs in peace.

There have been no religious wars in Chinese history. There is a cultural understanding of philosophy and religion. The Chinese believe all creatures of the universe are created by the One, call it what you may. Whether one is a follower of Buddhism, Zen or Taoism, eternal salvation is achieved through self-discipline and meditation leading to self-purification.

The eclectic nature of Chinese religious experience is evidenced by a recent archaeological find. The China Daily reported on June 19, 1987 that an ancient painted scroll was discovered in Southwestern China. The scroll was called "Hengting" which means "Spirit's Roadmap." The scroll, which is 15.6 meters long and 0.3 meters wide, contains features of Taoism and Buddhism. It is enhanced with features of Lamaism and the Tongba religion, a pantheistic worship of the gods of mountains, rivers, wind, and fire.

The Tao

To understand the teachings of Lao Tzu and Zhung Tzu, we must read a little from their works:

The Tao Te Ching by Lao Tzu

One

The Tao that can be voiced is not the eternal
Tao.
The name that can be stated is not the eternal
name.
The nameless is the beginning of Heaven and
Earth.
The named is the mother of ten thousand things.
Contemplate the "nothingness" to see its
mystery.
Contemplate the "existence" to see its
manifestations.
These two came from the same source but differ
in name.
Of all things profound, these are the deepest;
The gate to the mystery of all.

Two

In this universe, we can see beauty as beauty,
Because there is ugliness.
All recognize virtue as virtue,
Because there is evil.
Have and have not arise together.
Difficult and easy complement one another.
Long and short oppose each other.
High and low balance one another.
Music and sound harmonize each other.
Front and back follow one another.
So, the sage is working by non-action,
Teaching by not speaking.
Ten thousands things evolve ceaselessly.
Create, yet do not possess.
Work, yet do not take credit.
Accomplished, then forgotten;
therefore, it is eternal.

Eight

The highest virtue is like water,
It benefits ten thousand things and does not
strive.
It flows in lowly places that men reject.

So its nature is just like Tao.
It dwells everywhere.
In meditation, it is calm as water.
In dealings, benevolent.
In speech, truth.
In ruling, justice.
In business, competent.
In action, timing.
Such a man acts without fight and blame.

Thirteen

Honor and disgrace bring distress.
Misfortune is the human condition.
Why do honor and disgrace bring distress?
When honored, one is up,
When disgraced, one is down.
When one gains, distress,
When one losses, distress.
Why is misfortune the human condition?
The source of my misfortune comes
from having a body.
If I have no body,
How can I have misfortune?
When one surrenders oneself humbly to the
world,
Then, such a being can be entrusted in taking
care of the world.
When one loves the world as one's own self,
Then, such a being can be entrusted with the
sovereignty of the world.

Non-Action, Wu Wei

Lao Tzu's teaching is somewhat obscure and subtle by Western standards. He saw the whole universe as the perfect manifestation of Tao (or God, or Creator, or whatever you like). The essence of his teaching is summarized in two Chinese characters, "Wu Wei," which means non-action.

The principle of non-action does not mean to sit and do nothing. Rather, it is an understanding that all actions are gifts from Tao. Even man's internal organs function by the grace of Tao. Humans perform their daily actions by the grace and harmony of Tao. They act to the best of their abilities and leave the fruits of their actions to Tao. By giving up the attachment to the fruit of your action, you can then act in harmony with Tao.

The "fruit of your action" is the reward we all look for in our daily lives. It comes in different forms for different people. A cinema star is looking for the fruit of action in a new film contract. A writer is seeking the fruit of action in a new publication or a best seller. The fruit of a business person's actions may be a new promotion or higher profits. Politicians obviously measure their fruits in election results. It is not a principle of Taoism that one should not look for or expect the fruit; rather, it is that you should first act in harmony with nature; you should give your best effort and then forget about it.

Many Chinese have learned that the way to get by is to do nothing. Unfortunately, as with most profound scriptures the world over, men not spiritually equipped to comprehend the eternal verities which lie hidden in their writings misinterpret them for popular consumption. Lao Tzu's teachings have not escaped this fate. The harmony of action proposed by the concept of "non-action" was construed literally to be a call to not act.

The Chinese have practiced non-action for over two thousand years and truly believe that the more you do, the more trouble you bring down upon yourself. This corruption of the concept of "non-action" has contributed to the decline of Chinese society and its scientific advancements. If frustrated in dealings with the Chinese because of their lack of action, understand they are simply practicing the philosophy of "non-action."

The Teaching of Confucius

Confucius was born in 551 B.C. during the Spring-Autumn Period, when China was deeply divided by warring states and feudalism. Confucius tried to establish law and order by teaching the rulers they should rule with benevolence and justice and that the people should obey and respect them. At the time, no one listened to him. It was not until later generations that the rulers discovered the advantage of popularizing Confucius' teachings. They saw them as a method to control the people and set a uniform standard for respect and obedience.

The intention of Confucius was to re-establish law and order in a chaotic and broken country, but it was usual for the rulers to pay little attention to the first part of Confucius' teaching which stated they must govern with benevolence and justice. The result was two thousand years of political and social repression. The effects are still strongly felt in most parts of Asian society.

The foundation of Confucius' teaching is the proper conduct of each individual, also called "Dharma." His teachings cover how to serve society and how to perform the daily duties befitting one's station while learning to understand and become in tune with the Tao and Heaven. He taught that only when a man learns to cultivate his own virtue can he expand his concern to the family, the country, and the world. He taught what you do not wish done unto you, do not do unto others; a complementary manifestation of the Golden Rule. He stated:

The man who is full of wisdom and sees the Tao clearly has no doubts in his heart. The man who is full of virtue and benevolence has no selfish thoughts; therefore, he examines himself with no guilt. The brave man is in harmony with the truth and virtue; therefore, there is no fear within.

The virtuous man is full of Tao, such that within every word he speaks there is the essence of the Truth (Tao). The one who can speak skillfully, with seemingly sweet words, is not necessarily a virtuous man. The benevolent one, his whole heart full of eternal Truth with no self-interest, when his duty of life is called upon, will fulfill it at all costs. The courage is naturally within him. But a brave man will fight because of his temper or anger or to serve his pride, not necessarily to be benevolent.

When you are poor, having great difficulty clothing and feeding yourself and yet have no resentment or hatred in your heart, it is most difficult. When you are rich and full of wealth yet you can be contented and have no pride, this is easier to do.

When you are examining yourself in every movement, every word, and every action, you will make very few mistakes.

A learned man is very careful and timid in every word he says; but in action, he works very swiftly and is not lazy.

The virtuous man is not alone; his virtues will ever be his companions.

Zung Yung

Confucius' teaching is preserved in a book called Zung Yung "Zung" means center; "Yung" means eternal. It was thought by Confucius' students that years after his death this teaching would be misunderstood by future generations. It was therefore written so people might read his original words and rediscover the truth. The book of Zung Yung contains an important teaching:

Split many times from the middle, it becomes ten thousand things. In the end it will be united again into one Truth. If this Truth is let loose, it will fill the whole universe, but when you fold this Truth, it will hide in the smallest and most secret place. The essence of this Truth is endless. This is the True knowledge. The learned individual should contemplate and meditate upon this. The knowledge will reveal itself. When you take this true knowledge to all the aspects of your daily life, there is an endless supply.

1700 years later in the South Sung Dynasty, Chu Tzu edited a collection of four books on Confucianism. While doing so, he said: "All ten thousand things under the sky are nothing but consciousness. If you do not contemplate on this consciousness, what you have is only the limited knowledge. If you understand this principle of consciousness within all things, then all knowledge can be interchanged. This is the essence of knowledge."

"Zung Yung," called the middle path, has been misinterpreted as an indecisive, non-committal way. The result is that it has been used throughout the centuries to justify the idea that human life is cheap and that, in order to secure a position that will afford longevity, it is best to select the middle path: a non-committal position. The Chinese have often justified ignorance by using the words of Confucius to fit their needs.

During a business encounter with the Chinese, don't be surprised by a non-committal, indecisive person. Just know he is the product of two thousand years of Confucianism.

The Influence of China's Philosophy on the Japanese and Korean Societies

Both Japan and Korea have been deeply influenced by the Chinese way of thinking. Both societies respect Confucianism. The Japanese learned it well and established an orderly society based on obedience, discipline, and strong family commitment. One consequence of this was social repression at all levels of Japanese society. The Koreans have also created a society based on order and obedience, and along with it, social and political repression. The Chinese people have endured repression for thousands of years.

China, Japan, and Korea have each adapted and interpreted the wisdom of Chinese philosophers. The following two stories, the first Chinese, the second Japanese, demonstrate a strong similarity in the two countries' values.

A man named Sei Weng owned a beautiful mare, which the village people praised. One day this beautiful horse disappeared. The village offered sympathy to Sei Weng at his misfortune in losing his prize possession. Sei Weng said, "That's the way it is." A few days later his lost horse came back with a beautiful wild stallion. The village congratulated him for his surprising good fortune. Sei Weng said, "That's the way it is." Some time later, Sei Weng's only son was riding the stallion and he fell off the horse and broke his leg. The village people once again expressed their sympathy at Sei Weng's misfortune. Sei Weng again said, "That's the way it is." Then, a war started. All the young males of the village were drafted and sent to battle. Sei Weng's son was spared, however, because he had a lame leg. The village people were amazed at Sei Weng's good luck. His son was the only young man left in the village. Sei Weng kept his same attitude; despite all the turmoil, gains and loses, he gave the same reply, "That's the way it is."

The Japanese story concerns a young monk, Hakuin, who lived all alone in a little farm village. He meditated and followed his spiritual disciplines. He was not involved with a worldly life and was praised by his neighbors. A beautiful young girl who also lived in the farm village turned up pregnant. The girl's family asked her who the father of her child was. The girl cried and said, "Hakuin, the monk." The family went to Hakuin and criticized him. They condemned him for the dishonorable thing he had done. The young monk said, "Is that so?" When the baby was born, the girl's family gave the newborn son to Hakuin to raise. The monk took the boy and raised him as his own, still practicing his spiritual, isolated life. Hakuin never proffered an explanation for what had happened. Years passed with the village people despising the monk for being a person of no virtue. At long last, the young girl's conscience could stand it no more. She told her family that the father of her child was not the monk, but rather it was another young man of the village. Everyone went to the monk and apologized to him for abusing and dishonoring him for so many years. The monk said, "Is that so?" And uttered no other words.

The Japanese, Chinese and Korean Relationship

Recently at a meeting I was attending, an American lady came to me and asked if it were true the Koreans do not like the Japanese. She said she had been told this by a Korean businessman at a party she had attended the previous night. I told her that in my experience there still exist residual resentments among certain individuals. Koreans as a general rule do not like the Japanese. Japan conquered and occupied Korea during the early part of this century, and this experience has left bitter feelings with the Koreans.

Even though throughout history China has been in and out of Korea, their relationship has been much more relaxed. Although China sometimes took on the role of protector of Korea, it has more often taken on the role of conqueror. But once the battles were won, the Chinese have had a tendency to return home since they liked their homeland better.

The Japanese have had a different style and philosophy entirely. A hundred years ago, Japan decided to permanently occupy Korea in order to use Korea's natural and human resources to support the expansion of Japan. The methods used to control the Korean people were excessively cruel. The pride and spirit of the Korean people are strong. The more pressure put on by the Japanese, the more they rebelled. To this day, the fear of economic or military domination by Japan still lingers in the hearts and minds of the Korean people.

From the late 1800's to the end of World War II and the unconditional surrender by Japan, the Imperial Japanese government had essentially the same plan for China as they had for Korea. The Chinese people too have difficulty forgetting the actions of the Japanese.

My mother is from the Manchu area (Northeastern China). Japan took control of that area as early as the end of the last century. My mother told me that, in her home town, the path to the Japanese police station was clearly identified by a trail of blood on the ground. She, as a young child, had to pass by it each day on her way to school. She told me that traveling from one point to another was often a very dangerous thing. The Japanese would interrogate and often torture travelers right on the railway platform if their identification papers had the slightest hint of irregularity.

Although both my parents can speak Japanese fluently, having received their formal education in Manchu and Japan, to this day they will speak no Japanese under any circumstances. Even though it is sometimes advantageous in business to speak Japanese with Japanese people, they will not break this rule.

The older Chinese people lived through the occupation of China by the Japanese. The younger Chinese learned of the Japanese brutality from their parents and from history. The Chinese people as a whole still bitterly resent the brutal actions of the Japanese in China. However, a foreigner will seldom hear this resentment verbalized.

The Asian people share many similarities. Yet complex feelings and emotions, developed throughout their history, and especially the last hundred years, weave among them complicated and intricate relationships.

4 THE INNER CHINESE

There is a Chinese aphorism which states: "One should not display the family shame to an outsider." For this reason, the inner workings of the Chinese mind have been hidden from the Westerner. In this chapter, I will be revealing some of the collective Chinese family shame. What will be revealed will appear to many Westerners as prejudicial and steeped in vague and unfounded generalization. I want to make clear at the outset that the opinions expressed here are not the author's, but are rather a compilation of the writings of both well-known and obscure Chinese social critics.

Chinese Class Systems

There are four classes in traditional Chinese society. These classes have existed in stasis for thousands of years. The scholar is on the highest tier, followed by the farmer, laborer, and merchant.

In the old Chinese system, only the scholars could serve in government. It was therefore the goal of each Chinese to master the history and teachings of the great scholars (Lao Tzu, Zhung Tzu, Han Fei Tzu, Confucius) so that he might have a chance to serve as a government official or even as an assistant to the Emperor. Eventually, the emphasis on thinking and de-emphasis on productive labor contributed to the economic and political decline of China.

The merchant historically occupied the lowest position in the social structure. If in one's ancestral history there is a merchant, it is almost impossible to rise above that position in society. The first emperor of the Han dynasty, who ruled from 206 B.C. to 195 B.C., ordered the merchant class not to wear silk or ride in a vehicle, and levied an extremely heavy burden of taxation on the merchants. However, the Han dynasty was not the first to oppress the merchant class. Even as far back as the Chin dynasty (221 B.C. to 206 B.C.) there was an attempt to wipe out this "lowly class of peddlers".

The Chinese Communist government has tried to elevate the status of the uneducated laborer and suppress the prestige of the scholar, but class prejudices ingrained over the course of twenty centuries cannot be changed by decree. I once toured a successful hog farm in China. The farm was very profitable and was run only by the women of the household, while the men worked for the government. Even though the hog farm was more lucrative, the men held desk jobs because they wanted to be considered members of the scholar class.

There are the beginnings of a fifth class today in China: a combination of the merchant and scholar. This is a direct result of the need today for merchants to be well-educated in order to succeed in the complex business world of the twentieth century. Unlike the old time haggler in the market place, today the international merchant must often be a financier, accountant, and diplomat as well as a possessor of old- style trading skills. He may need to be an expert in one or more complicated subjects. These entrepreneurial merchants command a lot of respect because of their combined scholarly and business skills.

The Northern Chinese versus Southern Chinese

The Chinese feel strongly that there is a great distinction between the Northern and Southern Chinese, and each have strong patriotic ties to their respective geographical areas. The following characterizations exemplify the differences between the Northern and Southern Chinese.

The Northern Chinese tend to be large, strong, and stocky. The Southern Chinese tend to have a relatively smaller frame and less strength. Southern women are generally more delicate and are often famous for their beauty.

Lin Yu Tang said about the Northern Chinese that they are generally open, direct, candid, sincere, hot tempered, and hard working. They have a keen sense of humor, clothe themselves simply, and are good soldiers. In fact, until the 1900's, most Chinese military leaders and rulers were from the North. The Southern Chinese are smooth, often devious, and very intelligent. They like elegant sports and excel in trade and commerce.

The temperamental difference between the Northern and Southern Chinese can be recognized clearly in their poetry. The Northern poetry is straightforward and powerful. What it lacks in grace, it makes up in candor. The poetry of the Southern Chinese is more lyrical and descriptive, filled with tender emotions.

From the Western point of view, the Northern Chinese seem to make better negotiating partners than the Southern Chinese. The straightforward Northern attitude makes it easier to determine their objectives. The Southern Chinese often have hidden agendas, making it difficult to work through all the camouflage and smoke to the heart of the project.

What the Chinese Think of Themselves

Perhaps because philosophy is so important in individual lives, everyone in China is half philosopher. They spend a great deal of time examining their faults as a people and a nation. There have been a great many books on this theme recently published. They point out many negative qualities and harshly criticize the Chinese character.

What you are about to read may surprise you. It is a description of the beliefs the Chinese people hold about themselves. Many reputable Chinese scholars have written books about the Chinese character. The statements presented here are accurate summaries of their collective writings. While you may interpret many of these character traits as shortcomings, keep in mind that you are using a different cultural ruler -- that is, what may seem bad in the Western culture is not necessarily so in the Chinese culture. You may find some of these statements surprisingly frank. Remember, however, that among the Chinese, they are commonly held to be true.

Creative Interpretation of the Law

For thousands of years, the Chinese have learned and developed very special ways for taking care of business. As previously mentioned, Chinese people have described themselves as being sometimes slippery and tricky.

Here is a true story that demonstrates how the Chinese overcome obstacles to accomplish their business. Unlike Westerners, the Chinese do not like to fight the system. They would rather work around it, allowing the system to remain intact.

In the 1920's, the central government in Nanjin published a law ordering all Chinese government offices to move out of the Shanghai foreign territory. The high officials in Shanghai felt this law created a great deal of inconvenience, because most of the ministers had homes in the Shanghai territory. In addition, closing the office would mean a loss of employment for many people which would cause much hardship.

These officials did not, however, request that the central government reconsider the law, nor did they express the potential problems in its execution truthfully. Their solution, which was a bit more creative, was simply to change the names of the government offices from those that identified them as official government offices to nebulous names such as the "Trading Management Company." The total cost was twenty yen for each new sign on an office's front doors. No one lost his job. No one lost face. The central government was satisfied and the government administrators were happy.

This story is a classic example of how the Chinese circumvent authority without defying it. Foreigners often find out the hard way that the Chinese take the same attitude toward contracts and agreements.

Peace-Loving

Because the Chinese live in an agricultural society, they have been traditionally bound to the land. War for any reason is considered undesirable because it destabilizes an agricultural society. Therefore, the Chinese are a peace-loving people. Before the current government came into being, China was carved up like a great Christmas turkey by Britain, France, Germany, etc.

During World War II, the Japanese controlled the greater portion of China for eight years. Even though it has often been China's fate to be war torn, the people are not war-like. They have reacted to circumstances created either by foreign invasion or the ambitions of an internal strong man.

Contentment

The Chinese believe circumstances experienced in one's life are the result of fate. Consequently, the more you fuss with it, the worse it will get. One should accept things as they are. A consequence of this way of thinking is often a lack of initiative.

Endurance

Throughout history, the Chinese have endured hardships beyond the imagination of the Westerner. This has instilled a strength of character in the Chinese people. It has also created a great tolerance to the injustices thrust upon the individual by government and society. The Chinese have learned to accept life and authority.

Slippery and Tricky

This is perhaps the Chinese characteristic that frustrates Westerners most often. The Chinese have learned techniques of survival because survival has traditionally been difficult in their society. The Chinese say: "Of 36 strategies, escape comes first," and, "A good man never fights a losing battle." There are many heroes in Chinese history who repeatedly escaped and ultimately won the war. There are also heroes in Chinese history who insisted on the principle of fighting and, therefore, fought a losing battle and lost their lives. They are still admired for their courage and integrity, but in daily practice, most Chinese much prefer survival versus a heroic death.

Lack of Innovation

The Chinese once led the world in inventions and innovation, but generations of suppression and an inadequate educational system have left the Chinese people lacking the individual initiative required for innovation. Chinese society often tames the spirit of the most resourceful and superior individuals rather than encouraging the sometimes erratic fire of creativity.

Mooching

Mooching among the Chinese is a popular and accepted form of behavior. In some circumstances, it is expected. This is evident at the marketplace. If a Chinese purchases four eggs and some greens from the vegetable seller, it is expected the merchant will throw in something for free, perhaps some green onions. The Chinese grow up with this; children witness it at the market with their families.

This principle extends to international trading. The Chinese often expect something to be tossed in for free when they buy goods. It is important to build in a small profit margin to cushion the possibility of mooching by Chinese trading partners.

The Chinese also like to discount a seller's price. The Westerner may think a professional should give a fair price and stick with it. In China, however, everyone is trained to bargain, starting in childhood. The Chinese sometimes bargain simply for the sake of bargaining. They believe, though, that the poor should pay a little less for a product. And, since China is a poor country, the Chinese generally feel they should pay less on the international market and that extra components should be added to the original product as a gesture of good will.

A plastic materials dealer from England told me that he always adds two to three percent to the price of his goods. This way, when the bargaining begins, he can give this margin to the Chinese, allowing them to save face.

The Chinese don't feel giving a little bit away is unprofessional; rather they see it as an act of good will and friendship. In Chinese-American negotiations, the Westerner is the rich friend and the Chinese is the poor friend. The Westerner is supposed to discount his product.

Andre Pierre, the unfortunate Frenchman from Chapter 1, cut his price dramatically at one point. Some felt his price-cutting was an unprofessional act. I think in the long run, though, he made the right decision. The discounts Andre Pierre gave the Chinese negotiators made them look good in front of their superiors and his company ultimately won the contract.

Avoidance of Involvement

The Chinese avoid involvement because it tends to bring responsibility along with it -- and responsibility often means accountability. In a Communist-Socialist society, there is no incentive to be burdened with unnecessary involvement. This belief is reflected in some common Chinese sayings. For instance, "Increasing involvement is not as good as decreasing involvement," and, "Expending a great deal of energy will only bring ill fate." Clearly, the message is: "Don't get involved."

Selfishness

Some of the Chinese people's tendency toward selfishness results from the material realities of their society. There is a classic saying that refers to food as God. Keeping in mind that China has always been a place of too many people and too few developed resources, the meaning behind this saying becomes more understandable. After all, having too little for too many is a tremendous hardship on a society, and it is natural that this should result in selfish tendencies among the people.

Another contributing factor is a misinterpretation of the ancient Chinese philosophy that teaches the importance of cultivating the Self to function totally in harmony with the Tao. The Self in the context of this philosophy refers to the Higher Self. Over time, however, this has been misinterpreted to mean the individual self. The result, rather than a striving to cultivate the spiritual Self, is simple selfishness.

Finally, selfishness is a logical consequence of the "avoid involvement" philosophy and results in the Chinese being most interested in individual benefits rather than the collective good.

Lack of Regard for Public Property

The selfish attitude of the Chinese has led to a total disregard for public property. The extent of damage and neglect inflicted upon public buildings in China is extreme. Even relatively new buildings can be seen in such a state as to cause disbelief among Westerners. This lack of regard for public property extends to spitting in public places and excessive littering. Even a Chinese official will tidy up the interior of his car by throwing trash into the street. People spit and throw trash onto restaurant floors and they don't give it a thought. This is not the case in hotels and restaurants that Westerners frequent, but is common practice in the places patronized by the Chinese.

Lack of Unity

Chinese leaders repeatedly proclaim that the Chinese people must unite. Even as children, the Chinese are taught that sand has no strength, only clay soil has strength. But Dr. Sun Yet-sen said the Chinese people are like a plateau of sand. In business or in government, there is no unity. Lines of communication often do not exist between the divisions, departments, and ministries. An American who doesn't understand this may introduce one Chinese official with whom he is negotiating to another, even though they work for different ministries. In my experience, more often then not this causes the Chinese a great deal of discomfort.

The Chinese have a saying, "The Heaven is high, the Emperor is far." It means "what I do in my little world is my business." While the central government in China plays one melody, the provincial and local governments are often singing a different tune altogether.

Lack of Communication

Chinese believe "trouble is born out of the words you speak," another old adage. Hence, if departments do not share a common interest, communication can only lead to unnecessary trouble. This is a common attitude in government departments in both China and Taiwan. The private sector tends to be more results-oriented, so this behavior is discouraged. But the bureaucracy is not oriented toward results as much as toward not getting oneself into trouble.

Consider the case of a Chinese commodity production division and an import/export division that shared a building and were both government-owned. Neither division communicated with the other. The production division produced, and the importer imported. There was no relationship between the two. The production manager did not inform the importer when the production facility was producing a commodity similar to one that the importer was buying from abroad. Additionally, the production division sometimes sought a market abroad to generate foreign exchange, rather than providing the commodity to the domestic market. Consequently, there was much duplication of effort and loss of revenue. This story illustrates how the interests of one's own department are often perceived as more important than the greater objective.

Disharmony of the Heart and Mouth

The heart and mouth of the Chinese are often not in harmony. What they say is often not what they mean. The Chinese speak idealistically, sometimes saying things that are not true. This is especially true when they speak humbly. For example, if a Chinese says he doesn't feel he is good enough for a particular responsibility, that he is unqualified, do not take him too literally. If a Westerner were to take him literally, he might make an enemy for life. When a Chinese says he is not good enough, he does not mean it. What he means is that he is humble. It is up to the listener to perceive the virtue in his humbleness and convince the speaker to accept him as the most capable person for the job. In this way, the listener will grant the Chinese a lot of face.

Impatience and Patience

Westerners think of the Chinese as long on patience. This is not quite true. Somehow, time appears to move more slowly in mainland China, although Taiwan and Hong Kong move at a more Western pace. Time has never been equal to money as it tends to be in the West. In China, money is money and time is time. The Chinese take everything slowly, perhaps because the faster you go, the more you have to do -- and this is not a scholarly way of being. When the scholar comes to work, he takes his time.

He may smoke a pipe while enjoying a cup of tea and engaging in a little discussion of past history and present gossip. Then he opens the day's paper, reading it thoroughly as he slowly sips his tea. When he has finished, he calls a meeting, understanding that the business at hand is urgent. Then, showing great wisdom, he says, "We should consider this further at a future date." He has put in a good day's work and it is time to go home.

These same men often lack patience in their daily lives. There are no lines, for instance, at the bus stop; they wait for the bus to arrive and then muscle their way in. They may even fight with the bus driver, then with each other for a seat on the bus. The same behavior is even displayed when boarding pre-assigned seating on an airplane where such behavior makes no sense whatsoever.

Often, because of this impatience, the Chinese choose not to follow the rules. The best example of this is in traffic. In 1987, the leading cause of death in China was by automobile accident. That is an incredible statistic if you consider how few Chinese own cars, but those who have driven through rush hour traffic in Hong Kong or Taiwan will not be surprised by this statement.

Americans witnessing this behavior may wonder what happened to the renowned Chinese patience. A client of mine, who had been traveling with me in China for over a month and had experienced his share of Chinese "patience," remarked that he saw China as a society in panic.

This is one of the contradictions in the Chinese culture. On one hand, the Chinese function as if time were eternal -- Americans often see this as patient behavior. On the other hand, in local social interaction, individuals act aggressively, selfishly, and panicky, which is obviously impatient behavior.

Jealousy

The Chinese believe that they have a greater capacity for jealousy than people of other nationalities. Many are jealous of others' success, especially their friends and competitors, and even people they don't know. But strangely, there is an unspoken rule that their jealousy be directed mostly towards each other -- within the Chinese community -- and not directed toward foreigners.

Strategy Oriented

Chinese are a strategy-oriented people. Strategy is an integral part of the culture. Situations which, in Western minds, are handled by 'intuition' or 'common sense' are the subject of formalized strategies in Chinese thought. Even young children learn strategies for dealing with a wide variety of everyday problems.

Worry Now

The Chinese feel that if you don't worry about the future, immediate trouble will descend upon you. Most Chinese would rather worry now about the possibility of future trouble than deal with it when the time comes. They start to "worry now" in hopes that they will have no worries in the future. As a result, many Chinese have difficulty enjoying the present. They plan for the future and are always worried about it. This contrasts sharply with their acceptance of fate once it arrives.

Lack of Work Integrity

Quality control is often a problem resulting from poor production and lack of work integrity. There is a classic saying, "Horse, horse, tiger, tiger." It means, "I am not sure if it is a horse or a tiger, but it has four legs and a tail." In other words, it will get by. This is an especially great obstacle in the area of international trade with China. The people in China often do not have the slightest idea of the standards of quality required in the international market and often feel that the foreigners fuss about nothing. However, it should be noted that, if a Westerner is willing to apply the necessary effort, a quality product can be manufactured.

Indecision

A classic example of this is how the Chinese chose their national anthem. On September 27, 1949, the Preparatory Committee, after 14 years of soliciting for a suitable anthem, declared "The March of the Volunteers" a temporary anthem. During the Cultural Revolution, there was a period when "The East is Red" was used as a substitute national anthem. In 1979, by order of the People's Congress, the lyrics were changed. In 1982, the Fifth Session of the Fifth National People's Congress resolved to restore the original 1935 version of "The March of the Volunteers" as the official anthem.

Decisions are often made with the word "temporary" attached to them. The Chinese say, "The sky has unexpected thunderstorms, and humans have unexpected misfortune." In other words, the state of all things is unpredictable, therefore temporary. Those engaging in business negotiations with the Chinese should expect that the Chinese may request changes at any particular phase of the work, even long after the contract is signed and work has begun.

Having Face or Losing Face

The fear of losing face is nothing more than the fear of having one's ego deflated. This can be caused by a broad range of things: having an expected promotion fall through, one's child failing an examination, one's daughter marrying a poor man, one's brother working in a lowly position, all the way down to receiving a gift that is inexpensive. The list goes on and on. The logical counterpart to this is that anything that enhances the ego and provides glory is considered "granting face."

In general, because of this attitude, the Chinese prefer doing business with very large companies with worldwide reputations. There are two reasons for this. One is security: the Chinese feel that large companies are more powerful and, therefore, more secure. The second, and more important, is pride. The Chinese do not want to be seen by their colleagues as ones who do business with small companies. That would mean losing face. When they do business with the largest and best of international companies, it makes them look good and they "gain face."

Judgmental

The Chinese have a saying, "Slap your face until it is swollen," so that you look fat. That is, to keep your neighbors from laughing because you are poor and therefore skinny, you slap your face until it is swollen, making you look fat, and therefore, rich.

Many overseas Chinese don't like to mingle with Chinese social groups. They feel that by exposing themselves unnecessarily to other Chinese, they risk exposing themselves to vicious criticism. This may be the hard for Westerners to understand because of their notions about the humble and self-effacing Chinese. In reality, Chinese often are vicious with each other. Envy of those favored by good fortune and contempt for the less fortunate are very powerful forces in the Chinese community.

I have lived in the United States for nearly twenty years. I have never joined or associated myself with any Chinese organizations or groups. I only associate with other Chinese on an individual basis. I am by no means peculiar in this regard.

When in China, I often find that my fellow Chinese try to measure me against their understanding of American wealth. They try to determine how rich or how successful

I am by American standards so they can judge me accordingly.

Fond of Gossip

Without gossip, the act of social judgment alone would not provide much entertainment. The Chinese have a saying, "The Chang family long, and the Li family short." It refers to the idea that they always have something to say about every family. The Chinese are always interested in what their neighbor is doing. They keep a close watch on each other, which results in a society totally lacking in privacy. When news goes out the door, it becomes public. And news of the individual family easily becomes public because China is so heavily populated. When news is good, glory and face is gained. When news is bad, face is lost.

Patriotic

The Chinese are extremely patriotic. They have, throughout history, loved their country. Through a multitude of rulers and ruling parties, patriotism has existed in the people's heart. No matter where in the world a Chinese may find himself, the motherland is held dear. When a beloved ruler dies, the Chinese react with the same emotion as if they had lost one of their own family.

Kuan-Xie and Ho-Tai

Kuan-Xie and Ho-Tai are important concepts to understand if one is to function well in Chinese society. Kuan-Xie literally means relationships; Ho-Tai means backstage. Together they refer to an individual's power base, the important people who support one's position. The more one can use influential relationships and big names to support a cause, the easier the path will be. Simple merit may not be enough to advance one's case. Once a Chinese high official sadly expressed, "In China, it does not matter how many laws and how much righteousness are on your side, without Kuan-xie, you have nothing. The same goes for the situation in which you have no laws to support you; yet, you can do anything if you have the right Kuan-Xie and Ho-Tai."

Anywhere in the world, influential contacts can be a great asset. But one needs to magnify their importance a thousand times to understand the significance of Kuan-Xie in China. For five thousand years, guilty individuals have been pardoned because of Kuan-Xie and the innocent have lost their lives because of lack of Kuan-Xie. The ignorant have been promoted and the able have been discharged. It is very rare for one to be judged solely by his abilities in China. All Chinese people are affected by Kuan-Xie and Ho-Tai or their lack of it.

The present regime has failed to abolish Kuan-Xie. Without it, traveling in China is nearly impossible. In China you cannot prepurchase tickets for trains or airplanes. If you make a trip from Beijing to Nanjin, then Nanjin to Xian, from Xian to Xiaman, and Xiaman to Hong Kong, you must purchase tickets for each leg when you arrive at each city. So, to travel any distance, one needs to know people throughout the country so they can purchase tickets for you. You must have the people in position at the right time at each station. If you don't, when you arrive, you must wait in line to obtain tickets for your next destination. But by then it may be too late to obtain a ticket for the desired train.

This is why one always sees peasants at the Beijing train station. Many destinations have no direct route, and Beijing is a common place to change trains. The peasants, most of whom don't have Kuan Xie, sleep in front of the station because they are trapped waiting for a train. It can take several days to get on the proper train. The system is so bad that even the simplest trip, not to mention important business travel, requires Kuan Xie.

This is true in all Asian societies. If you have an introduction or reference from the right person, you will receive a warm welcome. If you knock on the door cold, there is a distance created that is difficult to overcome. Western companies could save immeasurable work by being introduced by the right people. This is true elsewhere in the world, but it is not as necessary a prerequisite to doing business as it is in the East. Use Kuan Xie and your way will be made smooth.

Regional Identity

The Chinese recognize a strong bond to village and province. There is an instant rapport when you discover someone is from the same province or village, and this relationship plays an important role in the game of Kuan-Xie and Ho-Tai.

In large cities like Los Angeles and New York, Chinese from the same province or city and those who share the same surname form associations. The Chinese believe that those who share the same surname are from the same ancient family. Although some Chinese, as I mentioned, stay apart in order to avoid being the target of gossip, others enjoy the game. They socialize together and support each other, and have fun fighting within their own association and with other associations and groups.

Family Ties

The Chinese people's strong family ties are the pillars of Chinese civilization. It is these ties that have allowed the people to survive China's seemingly unceasing internal wars, and it is these ties that make the Chinese civilization indestructible.

Hao-She

In his book, <u>My Country and My People</u>, Lin Yu-Tang writes of one of the most common Chinese male behavior: Hao-She, which means "love-sex." For thousands of years, the Chinese practiced polygamy. Today polygamy is against the law, but that does not stop many from having extramarital sex -- especially those who are wealthy or in high positions. It is still a popular practice.

In Taiwan and Hong Kong, mixing sex with business is often considered a good business practice. A businessman may entertain clients in a place very much like a brothel. If a client fancies a particular girl, arrangements are made for that girl to accompany the client overnight. An American friend of mine once told me about a visit he made to Taiwan. His Chinese host wished to express his hospitality by sending a virgin girl to his hotel room.

Mixing sex with business is practiced only in all-male business circles. They feel that once the male circle of friends has played together, bonds are formed which make business deals easier to close. However, if there is a female executive among them, this form of entertainment is out of the question.

While these practices are common, not all Chinese men participate in them. In general, it has been said the Chinese man's attitude is that what his wife doesn't know won't hurt her. If he feels guilty about his infidelities, he may treat her better and this, he feels, is good for the family relationship. Many wives of Chinese businessmen accept the mix of sex and business as usual procedure. They ignore it and pretend it is not there.

Wife-Fearing

Unlike Japanese and Korean men, the Chinese have a common agreement that real men are wife-fearing. The first emperor of the Sui Dynasty (581 A.D.), Wen Di, united China after nearly two hundred years of civil war and division. Despite this accomplishment, it is maintained that he was so afraid of his wife that when she was angry, he would run to the mountains and hide, not returning until he had been notified that her anger had ceased. He was like a mouse in front of his wife, and a tiger in front of his enemies.

Emperor Tai Zong(626 - 649 A.D.) of the Tang Dynasty helped his father establish the Tang Dynasty by overthrowing the Suei Dynasty and initiated the beginning of China's Second Golden Era. History tells us that Fong, minister and advisor to Emperor Tai Zong, was most afraid of his wife. One day he could stand the pressure from his wife no more and he went to the Emperor for help. The Emperor told Fong to send his wife to him and he would put her in her place. Fong's wife appeared before the Emperor and they exchanged a few words, whereupon, Emperor Tai Zong reported back to Fong that he too was afraid of Fong's wife and in the future Fong should just obey her.

In China, queens have ruled the entire country. There have been female warriors who challenged male opponents on the battlefield. Women gave their lives during the twentieth century revolutions. In the Chinese family structure, the highest position is often held by the woman of the house. This contradicts the common American myth that Chinese women are subservient and powerless -- that phase of Chinese history occurred only during the Ming dynasty (1368 - 1644 A.D.)

The Chinese classic novel, Dream of the Red Chamber, describes this vividly. Among the princesses of the Tang Dynasty, 23 married two times, and 4 married three times. In China, any woman who is capable of reaching for power may obtain it. Chinese women seldom fight for their rights, but they are very aware of them.

Humor

The Chinese sense of humor is unique to their culture. What seems funny to the Chinese does not seem to translate well enough to share with foreigners. Chinese humor has become an antidote for the unbearable suffering that has filled the common folks' daily life in this ancient country's history. This quality has allowed China to survive throughout the centuries against all domestic turmoil and foreign invasions.

For example, I was once chatting with some Chinese visitors during a long-distance trip in a minibus. We talked about the funny phrases that the Chinese use to describe the people from different parts of China, such as referring to those from the city of Tianjin as having "a mouth that can talk a dead man to life." This is because their regional trait seems to be that they talk so much. People from Beijing are judged by the other provinces to be as "slippery as oil," as Beijing is the traditional seat of political power, and that type of personality thrives in such an environment.

The citizens from Baoding, the home of one of the most famous military schools in China, are called "leg-huggers" because they have mastered the art of hugging each others legs (being promoted by their classmate friends) in their advancement up the rungs of the governmental ladder.

Such sayings do not offend the people being discussed for there is never any accusation of prejudice. We then moved the subject to our foreign invaders, Japan and

Russia. One Chinese said, "Japan has a very small house so they like to visit someone else's house and Russia has a large house but Russians don't like their house so they like to stay at their neighbor's house." We laughed about these descriptions of our past invaders.

Chinese do not often take themselves as seriously as the Japanese take themselves. The Chinese laugh about their hardship and disgrace and somehow they have the ability to transcend it.

The Ugly Chinese

The Ugly Chinese, written by Bo Yong and published in Taiwan, was an instant hit there. The book gives a vivid description of the Chinese people. It is an in-depth analysis of the Chinese through Chinese eyes. It does not present a very flattering image, but it is honest. The book was surprisingly well-received in mainland China as well. But the student riots in early 1987 resulted in the Chinese government tightening controls on expressions of liberal thought in China and the book became restricted material. It was barred from further publication or circulation.

Bo Yong was familiar with government repression. He had been arrested as a political activist because he was outspoken against the Taiwanese government. He said people like himself, under the current set of political circumstances, will always experience the same fate, be they Chinese in Taiwan or mainland China.

As Bo Yong sees it, the Chinese people are more a culture than a nationality. They are a group of people who share the same ancestors and culture. No matter what country a Chinese may be living in, he will always remain Chinese first and other Chinese will continue to see him as Chinese.

Bo Yong described the Chinese as dirty, messy, and noisy. In fact, the Chinese do have big loud voices. No one else in the world can compete with the loud voices of the Chinese. Bo Yong believes the Chinese use a loud voice because they are basically insecure. The louder they speak, the more righteous they seem.

The Chinese love to fight within their own nest. Bo Yong believes that this is the most important characteristic of the Chinese people. He wrote that one Japanese looks like a pig, while three look like a dragon. Each Chinese thinks he is a dragon and when three dragons get together, each one looks like a pig. This implies that, one Japanese may not be very impressive by himself, but when three Japanese get together, they create a very impressive force. The Chinese are just the opposite, and usually create petty internal disputes which leads them to look like a group of pigs.

The Chinese have a parable about monks: One monk scoops the water and drinks it; two monks carry the water back to the temple and divide it between them; when three monks get together, nobody has water to drink. This parable demonstrates Bo Yong's point: When three Chinese get together, there will be three different opinions and there will be three different decisions. He says that Chinese do not often agree and that they have no concept of cooperation, harmony or unity.

Another special characteristic of the Chinese, according to Bo Yong, is never admitting that they are wrong. NEVER. And because the Chinese do not admit they are at fault, they will do anything to cover a mistake. The Chinese have a saying, "Close the door and concentrate on faults." While this was meant as a means of introspection, Bo Yong believes that, in reality, the Chinese concentrate on others' faults, certainly not their own. Indeed, the Chinese will create more mistakes to prove that an initial mistake was not a mistake. They may create ten mistakes to cover one and 100 mistakes to cover the ten.

Bo Yong also talked about how foreigners do not understand that the Chinese mouth and heart are not the same. The Chinese may talk falsely with big, empty words and with a vicious tongue. What the Chinese say and what they mean may be two totally different things. When it is understood what is being said, it must be translated into what is really meant.

According to Bo Yong, if a Chinese is working in a foreign country and his boss is Chinese, he must be extremely careful. His boss will not promote him. Further, when the boss needs to cut back, he may fire the Chinese first to demonstrate that he is a truly fair person. If the worker does something wrong and gets turned in secretly by some unknown person, one of his Chinese friends probably did it.

Bo Yong speaks of the Chinese people's small-heartedness. If you look at them one time too many, you may "get a knife." I was on a train with a Chinese official. As we passed a cabin, a Chinese inside looked at my host. My host turned with great anger and said, "What are you looking at?" This is a typical reaction.

In Western society, you often shake hands after a fight and are friends. In China, it takes three generations to get revenge.

Bo Yong continued to say that the Chinese will never have equality among themselves, because in Chinese thinking, if you are not my master, then I am your master. There is always an inferior-superior, master-slave relationship.

This inferior-superior relationship is not limited to others. Bo Yong strongly believes the Chinese have this same struggle within. He observed that, while the Chinese behave absolutely arrogantly, they are feeling totally inferior at the same time.

Chinese are very fearful people. If you ask a Chinese business associate for his name so you can send something to him, he may respond by telling you to just send it to the department. Nobody in the mainland Chinese business world likes to be identified. They are afraid that if they are identified something bad will happen to them.

Bo Yong observed that the Chinese copy anything new in a foreign society and flavor it with their own special characteristics. For example, the Chinese translate Western world democracy into a philosophy of "you do what you wish, I do what I wish." This is not a far-fetched translation, since the Chinese characters for democracy translate literally into "individual" and "master."

These are just a few of the characteristics Bo Yong addresses in his book. I believe Bo Yong's views result from a great love for the Chinese people. He hopes that by bringing to the surface these cultural faults, he may raise awareness so they can be corrected.

Zheng Ren

"Zheng" means to turn something upside down, to reorganize it; it also means to cause hardship. "Ren" means human being. "Zheng Ren" means to cause somebody a hardship by reorganizing.

This is a concept unique to the Chinese culture. It refers to creating something out of nothing in order to cause harm, and it is an integral part of Chinese society. Anywhere there is a group of Chinese -- China, Hong Kong, Taiwan -- you will find Zheng Ren, especially in government and political circles.

There are government employees in China who do nothing. They just read the newspaper, drink tea and receive their salaries. They are not bad people; they mind their own business. They might not be productive, but they are not destructive.

Other government employees do not read the newspaper, drink tea or go to work. They dedicate their whole lives to Zheng Ren. They make something out of nothing and destroy other people with it, all for their own advancement.

These people believe that making somebody else look bad makes them look better. They destroy someone and they receive rewards for it. The technique these people use is covered in the 36 Strategies (see Chapter 8). It is Strategy 7, Something from Nothing.

By creating something from nothing, these people are self-appointed watchdogs for the government. Without them watching and creating trouble, China would be a much more productive place.They interfere with others who are engaged in productive enterprises.

There is a true story about a man who was tried and sentenced to life in prison for crimes that his accusers said he committed. As a result, his family left him and he went insane. Although he was later exonerated and released, the people who had falsely accused him had been promoted precisely because they had accused him. They had, in the government's eyes, done society a great service by removing this harmful man. These people kept their promotions, even after the man was cleared of all charges. They were untouchable.

I wish I could say that only a small portion of the Chinese government staff spend most of their time practicing Zheng Ren. Unfortunately, a large portion of the government workers in both China and Taiwan spend a great deal of energy finding creative new ways of fault-finding and back-stabbing.

When there is a concentrated force of these self-appointed watchdogs and they are led by a strong leader, it can result in phenomena like the Cultural Revolution. I once asked a Chinese friend, "What was the Cultural Revolution?" He answered simply, yet with the most descriptive and powerful truth: "The Cultural Revolution was the whole country, everyone, all of its productive forces, all becoming politicians."

During the Cultural Revolution management and workers reduced the country to chaos. Everyone was proving that they were the true daughters and sons of Mao's revolution by being more vicious than anyone else. Chinese politicians displayed their talents of Zheng Ren by finding ways to bring down whoever was in power. Those that were the most vicious were promoted.

These are the same games the Chinese have been playing on a small scale since the beginning of history, limited in ancient times to the players in the royal imperial court. Mao found a way to expand the game into the whole of China, to include one billion players. This was where Chinese ugliness hit its peak.

Mao Zedong -- A Master of Zheng Ren

Mao spent enormous amounts of time studying the power struggles in China's history. He studied the ways in which Zheng Ren, which has been played throughout Chinese history, was used in the old Chinese court. He learned to master every aspect of the written and unwritten rules of Zheng Ren to consolidate his power.

He knew how to use others to eliminate his enemies. People like the Gang of Four acted as his mad dogs, doing the barking and biting.

Mao surrounded himself with people who were experts in undercutting other people's power by cleverly creating something out of nothing. Therefore, brilliant people like Zhou Enlai, Liu Shaoqi and Deng Xiaoping, the best China had to offer, were unable to contribute to the reconstruction of China.

An old party member with a new liberal perspective who knew Mao Zedong vividly expressed his view of Mao to me by saying that Mao was good at two things: guerrilla warfare, which got him into power, and Zheng Ren, which kept him in power. However, as far as knowing how to reconstruct China, Mao was inept.

War enabled Mao to show off his talent at guerrilla warfare. He constantly prepared for war and couldn't wait to involve China in wars, such as those with Korea and Vietnam. In China itself, instead of creating meaningful economic reconstruction, he kept the labor force busy digging caves in the mountainsides in the event of an invasion of the mainland, which never occurred.

Mao and Muo Dun

Muo Dun is a concept Mao developed and wrote about in 1939. The concept of Muo Dun was studied and memorized by everyone. Any Chinese currently over the age of 20 studied this material during the Cultural Revolution. "Muo" here means the spear that soldiers use to fight. "Dun" means the shield the soldier uses to protect himself. The spear and the shield, Muo Dun, are forces that oppose each other. The spear is for attack, the shield is for defense.

Natural phenomena are composed of opposing forces: action and reaction, positive and negative. In the dynamics of human relations there are also fundamental opposing forces. Mao believed you can control any situation by identifying the opposing forces and applying your effort where it has the greatest leverage to tip the course of events in your direction. Mao later created the Cultural Revolution by magnifying the principle of Muo Dun to apply to the whole country.

When it comes to business negotiations, you will have a greater advantage if you understand that some of your adversaries participated in the Cultural Revolution, an elaborate and prolonged negotiation for power and often survival. This experience has educated them in methods of deception beyond most Westerner's capacity to understand.

In Summary

All these characteristics manifest themselves differently in political, social, and economic environments. While some of these are easily identified as universal, the Chinese refer to them as "Chinese Trademarks."

Now that you have some insight into the sociological traits and their basis in history, you can begin to understand how these characteristics affect the everyday dealings you will have in your business with the Chinese.

5 THE CHINESE CONCEPT OF BUSINESS

Use History as a Mirror

It is not difficult to understand why American business people and politicians often feel frustrated when dealing with Asians. Americans sometimes refer to Asian behavior as unprofessional and inconsistent. As a matter of fact, Asians follow a much more definite set of rules than do their American counterparts.

Asia is rich in a history which, unlike Western history, is centered more on people and less on events. The people's thought processes and their psychological development have been subjects of extensive study. The study of history itself is far more general in China than in the West because the examination system is so important to individual advancement among members of the scholar class. A thorough knowledge of history is essential to success in the examinations.

There is a popular old Chinese saying: "Use history as a mirror." Today's Asian leaders do just that, going back to ancient knowledge, seeking guidance for their day-to-day business and political affairs from the examples of history. In order to examine the roots of Asian business philosophies, we need to examine these same sources.

Since the re-opening of China in the late 1970's, the Chinese have been criticized in the West for unconventional business and political behavior. But the strategies that underlie the behavior of the mainland Chinese are not very different than those of the people of Japan, Korea, Taiwan or Hong Kong. Because international business has a longer history in those countries, they have had an opportunity to adapt their negotiating techniques for use in dealing with the Western world. Their techniques are not really different than the original concepts and strategies the Chinese use, but are simply an updated version.

Regardless of the criticism the Westerner might have of Chinese ways, he must acknowledge that China is the oldest civilization on Earth and is once more beginning to assert its position of importance in the international community. China survived when other civilizations vanished from the surface of the Earth. When one looks deep enough, one will discover the motor that drives the behavior of the Chinese. Perhaps some of the confusing, unprofessional, and seemingly inappropriate behavior of the Chinese are merely a reflection of the naive and arrogant attitudes of some Western businessmen and politicians who measure the whole universe by Western standards. In the following topics, we will explore some of the unspoken motivations of Asian business people with stories which illustrate their application.

The Marketplace is a Battlefield

The Chinese aphorism, "Shang chang ru zhan chang," literally translates as: "The marketplace is a battlefield." This is how the Chinese people view the importance of success in the business world. The success of a small business affects the livelihood of a few families. The success of a large business affects the livelihood of thousands of families. Today, of course, the success of the entire country's economy directly influences the survival and well-being of the nation. The Chinese understand the true nature of business competition. They see it and call it as it is: "Shang chang ru zhan chang."

The Japanese have always been the greatest disciples of Chinese wisdom. When it comes to the perfect execution of this principle, the pupil has surpassed the master. The limited natural resources of Japan have been cause for much concern among Japanese leaders. Japan's invasions of China and Taiwan in 1874 and during World War II were actions motivated by the need for territorial expansion to ensure the survival of their isolated island civilization. Following WWII, Japan got smart and remembered the old Chinese saying, "Shang chang ru zhan chang" and began making a steady practice of it. Through the marketplace, Japan has finally secured its national survival. It has demonstrated the truth of the Chinese saying: "The highest victory is to win a war without battles."

Utilization of War Strategies in Business Practice

The use of superior strategies in the battlefield is the course every military leader should take. The leader must study and master the art of manipulation and use it creatively. An almost endless succession of battles and wars have been waged throughout China's history. Five thousand years of recorded history serve as a guide for political and military leaders. Transferring war strategies into a business philosophy is a natural transition.

The Chinese believe all elements of life are interconnected. The wisdom that guides the general in battle is the same wisdom by which the politician maneuvers his power. It is this wisdom which guides all of Mankind in their daily lives. The Chinese apply a systematic study of fundamental human behavior to every aspect of life, including family relationships, public relationships in a work environment, and strategies to gain promotions and recognition.

The History of Bing-Fa, The Art of War

Bing means soldier. Fa means skill. Since the Chinese believe the marketplace to be a battlefield and that life is a series of battles, mastering Bing-Fa (skillful soldiering) is an essential course for survival. Bing-Fa is a living knowledge; it is the goal of every Chinese to be able to apply this knowledge to his daily life. Chinese rulers have always placed a high importance on mastering Bing-Fa. Around 220 A.D., China was divided into three parts and ruled by three separate rulers, the time of Three Kingdoms. The last words spoken from the deathbed of Liu Bei, one of the three rulers, were to his young son instructing him to master Bing-Fa. The Prime Minister and Commander-in-Chief, Zu Ge Liang, copied the old military war strategies by hand and taught the young master personally.

The historical document, Han Books, was written during the period 206 B.C. to 24 A.D. The collection Yi-Wen Series contains a total of 596 books. Of these 596 books, 53 record knowledge of military strategy (Bing-Fa). At the time these books were written, there was no printing technology. The books were written or carved on wood or bamboo strips. That the knowledge of Bing-Fa was very important to the Chinese is demonstrated by the number of handwritten books dedicated to the subject.

Emperor Chin, in 221 B.C., ordered the burning of all books in China. In the early Han Dynasty (206 B.C.), there were 182 Bing-Fa books which escaped Emperor Chin's fires. There must have been many more Bing-Fa books before the Chin Dynasty, during the time of the Warring State (481-221 B.C.) and the Spring-Autumn period (772-480 B.C.), which did not escape this fate.

Bing-Fa was originally set down by Tei Wang Gung. His expert military strategy helped establish the Zhou Dynasty in 1122 B.C. Tei Wang Gung wrote two books on the subject of Bing-Fa. The fundamental philosophy of Bing-Fa was to creatively use a set of basic principles in military maneuvers: "Lead the enemy to relaxation and neglect. Politically isolate the enemy. Seek the support of allies, and wait for a favorable opportunity to conquer."

Influence of Philosophy

Bing-Fa is not just the knowledge of military maneuvers. It combines political, economic, cultural, and philosophic strategies. During the five hundred years from the beginning of the Spring-Autumn period to the end of the Warring States (772-221 B.C.), the techniques of conquest evolved from simple battle plans to complex, multifaceted and multidimensional strategies. This is the time when Chinese philosophers flourished. Zhung Tzu, Lao-Tzu, Han Fei Tzu, Confucius, and Meng Tzu, all lived and taught during this period.

Among these philosophers, Lao-Tzu had the greatest influence on Chinese Bing-Fa. He taught that universal principles are only one, and the one becomes the many.

Lao-Tzu's Tao Te Ching, verse 42:
The Tao gives birth to the one.
One gives birth to two.

Two gives birth to three.
And three gives birth to ten thousand things.
The ten thousand things carry yin
and embrace yang.
By combining these forces, harmony is created.

The backbone of military strategy is the combined wisdom of Lao-Tzu's Tao Te Ching and the I-Ching (The Book of Changes). The origin of the I-Ching may be as old as the Five Emperors of the legendary period during the time of Fu Xi (2953- 2838 B.C.). The I-Ching is considered to be the first written book of wisdom, philosophy, and oracle and has acted as a guide for rulers and scholars throughout history. The I-Ching is the vehicle used for understanding the patterns of universal changes that govern all aspects of creation. It is the guidebook that directs all aspects of one's daily life, from family to business affairs. It is an advisor which reveals the best action to be taken at a given moment, in every decision and life event. It can be used everyday, both for spiritual exploration and daily life directions.

From observation of life comes the knowledge of Tao and I-Ching. Tao is the essence of Oneness, and the I-Ching is the everchangingness of that Oneness. So the combination of these two sources of knowledge allows one to understand the essence of the unchangeable and the everchanging. The ancients embraced the essence of Tao and I-Ching and discovered the natural rhythm of manipulative military strategies.

Some other famous Bing-Fa masters are Wu Tzu, Sun Bin, Zu Ge Liang, Su Chin, Chang Yi, Han Xin, and Sun Tzu.

At the present time, the most complete war strategy book is Sun Tzu's Bing-Fa. It was written by Sun Tzu in the fourth century B.C. and is one of the most popular Bing-Fa books among the Chinese people. This book was first translated into French in 1772 by a Jesuit missionary, J.J.M. Amiot (Sun Tzu, The Art of War, Confucius Publishing Co.), and has since been translated into many other languages.

Wide Popularity

Sun Tzu's Art of War is widely studied throughout Asia by political and business leaders. While the American is busy learning how to update management skills by reading books such as the One Minute Manager, the people of the East have never stopped contemplating and analyzing the ancient, timeless truths of Sun Tzu's Bing-Fa.

The influence of Chinese Bing-Fa is not limited to China, but extends to Japan, Korea, and other oriental countries touched by Chinese culture. People who deal daily with the Chinese people must master the knowledge and strategies of Bing-Fa. Takashi Yamamura is General Manager for Japan C. Itoh & Co., Ltd., which has 11 branch offices in China. I asked Mr. Yamamura whether he studied the Bing-Fa of Sun Tzu. He looked at me in utter amazement that I should have asked, and answered, "Of course."

Asian people enjoy matching wits with Americans. When they do business with Americans, they are usually in charge of the game since Americans are rarely aware that a game is being played.

In a meeting between Henry Kissinger and Chou Enlai, Secretary Kissinger made a comment that demonstrated an awareness of the strategies that Chou was employing with him. Chou complimented him by saying, "You are very smart." Kissinger replied, "You mean, smart for an American." Chou smiled and said nothing.

When the Chinese do business with each other, dealings often develop into a sophisticated contest. A Taiwanese diplomat once said, "When I am assigned overseas, life is so much easier and simple. When I am transferred back to my country, it is so complicated. Everyone PLAYS GAMES here."

Sun Tzu said, "Know yourself, know your opponents; one hundred battles, one hundred victories." Anyone dealing with Chinese businessmen or political figures must have a thorough understanding of Bing-Fa. Later, we will examine how the Chinese apply the principles of Bing-Fa to their business practices.

Love the Game

It is not necessary for Bing-Fa to be studied formally by Chinese people in order for them to understand the principle of its application. Because it is all around them from the day they are born, it becomes a part of their very soul. They are taking daily lessons in the art of maneuvering by simply existing in the elements of their environment. They learn quickly to love the game that they play so naturally. They practice with their family members, at their place of work or school, within their political party, and in every dimension of their life.

When I was fifteen years old, I discovered the pleasure of wearing beautiful clothes. In Taiwan at that time, there were no ready-made clothes. One purchased the material for garments and had them sewed. I had a limited budget and a yearning for lovely dresses. I had not studied war strategy, but my intuition showed me the shopkeeper's weakness that would be an asset to me.

The shopkeeper's weakness was a local superstition dictating he must sell to the first customer of the day because, if the customer left without making a purchase, the bad luck of poor earning would follow for the remainder of that business day. I spent many Sunday mornings waiting for the shop doors to open and the tactic worked well for me. Without realizing it, I was applying a sophisticated, classical battle strategy. As we bargained back and forth, I walked away many times and was called back to renegotiate. The shopkeeper served tea and we talked about his or her children, family affairs and general gossip. Making friends is one of the essential elements of a favorable bargaining and negotiation procedure. Remember, as mentioned in Chapter 1, the Chinese have to sell cheaper to their friends. Some times this took hours but, finally, the shopkeeper would say, "You are such a sweet, nice girl. I will sell this only to you at such a ridiculously low price. Don't tell anyone you bought this fabric at my place at this price." Of course, I also knew you couldn't really believe what the shopkeeper said. But I bought the material for clothes at a good price, and the shopkeeper made a sale to his first customer of the day plus earned a small profit.

I don't bargain with the shopkeepers anymore. I just let them charge me whatever they want since time and energy are much more important commodities to me now.

The following stories demonstrate how Bing-Fa can be applied to the circumstances of daily life.

Top Horse, Middle Horse, and Weak Horse

Sun Bin (exact birth date unknown) in the Period of the Warring States (476- 221 B.C.) was a genius in the art of maneuvering through military strategies. He wrote a Bing-Fa book which was lost for over two thousand years. It was rediscovered in 1972 in China's Shangdong Province's silver peacock mountain tomb. Unfortunately, the book was not complete.

Sun Bin's feet were chopped off by a jealous schoolmate who feared Sun Bin would be a great threat to his future position. Sun Bin was rescued by the Ambassador of Chi, and the great General Tian of Chi took Sun Bin as his confidant and advisor.

General Tian Ji of Chi often raced horses with the King and princes of Chi for entertainment. The wagering often involved large amounts of money. General Tian mentioned an upcoming horse race to Sun Bin. Sun Bin told General Tian he could guarantee winning the match and that General Tian should bet any amount he desired on the competition. Sun Bin was familiar with Tian's horses and knew their ability to perform. General Tian was nevertheless doubtful of Sun Bin's ability to guarantee a win because each of his horses matched up very evenly with one of the opponents horses.

Sun Bin divided the horses into three categories: best, middle, and worst. Sun Bin then told General Tian to race his worst horse against his opponent's best horse, to put his middle horse up against his opponent's worst horse, and finally to race his best horse against his opponent's middle horse. General Tian followed Sun Bin's advice and realized one loss, two wins and was declared the winner of the match, taking home the gold.

Story of Clay Stoves

Sun Bin was leading the army of Chi in a retreat from the army of Wei. The former schoolmate of Sun Bin, Pang Juan, who had ordered Sun Bin's feet chopped off, was the head of the army of Wei. Wei's army was larger and better equipped then the army of Chi. Sun Bin and General Tian discussed the situation. They knew from the past that the army of Wei was stronger than theirs and that the army of Wei considered the army of Chi inferior. The soldiers of the army of Chi were fearful of the army of Wei and the army of Wei knew it. Sun Bin and General Tian knew something had to be done. They looked for a way to turn the situation to their advantage.

When the army of Chi made camp after the first day's retreat Sun Bin ordered the soldiers to make 100,000 clay stoves (it was standard procedure for an army to construct temporary clay stoves when in the field). The soldiers wondered at the order. They certainly didn't need that many stoves but they obeyed and made the specified number. The army moved on. The next evening Sun Bin ordered the soldiers to make 50,000 stoves and on the third day he ordered 30,000.

The army of Wei observed that, as each day passed, the army of Chi had left behind fewer and fewer stoves. To the army of Wei it looked like the soldiers of the army of Chi were deserting, probably because they were cowardly and afraid of the army of Wei. The army of Wei therefore concluded that the army of Chi would never dare face them. In three day's time, the army of Wei had been led into the impression that two-thirds of the Chi soldiers had fled. The army of Wei grew arrogant and less cautious and quickened the pace of their pursuit. Sun Bin's former schoolmate ordered a small group to follow him and give chase to the army of Chi, confident that Chi's army had deteriorated to a small dispirited group. Sun Bin lay in wait to ambush the commander of the army of Wei. Just as he had predicted, his schoolmate fell for the trap and lost the battle as well as his life.

Eating Guest (Shi Ke)

Shi means "to eat" or "food." Ke means "guest." The feudal lords, who struggled to conquer each other during the Spring-Autumn and Warring States periods, sought help from Bing-Fa masters and philosophers. These people, often called "Eating Guests," were advisors and consultants. The name Eating Guests was derived from the fact that their livelihood was provided by the Court in exchange for their wisdom. The feudal lords and other officials all had Eating Guests to provide them with words of wisdom or brilliant strategies. They deliberated on problems and sought advice on how to conquer or avoid being conquered.

The peak period for these Eating Guests was during the time of Lu Bu Wei, who had 3000 in his court. Lu Bu Wei assisted the Lord of Chin to unite China, establishing the Chin Dynasty which ended the 500 years of China's warring states. Many of the strategies that have survived to today were formulated by these Eating Guests.

Today, one must be careful to determine who has the greatest influence on a given business decision. If you are dealing with the modern counterpart of the Eating Guest who might occupy a seemingly menial position during discussions, you run the risk of misdirecting your strategy.

In Conclusion

Bing-Fa wisdom has been tested for hundreds of generations during many dynasties. It has been integrated into every fiber of the Chinese social, economic, and political structure. The Chinese will tirelessly play the game of Bing-Fa, especially if they can see a reward at the end of the contest. A foreigner who thinks the Chinese are being unprofessional or erratic is simply not recognizing the systematic application of these ancient principles. Bing-Fa is a time-honored philosophy and the Western businessman who wishes to do business in China must recognize its application and learn how to deal with it.

In the next chapter, we will explore the heart of the elements that make up Bing-Fa.

6 THE ESSENCE OF WAR STRATEGIES

The Art of War (Bing-Fa) by Sun Tzu is the study of military strategy. Military strategy is not to be thought of as limited only to the maneuvering of troops. As a matter of fact, that is a rather small portion of it. Intelligent maneuvering of the human mind and a knowledge of how the mind functions can be used to create tactical advantages in all areas of human interaction.

A knowledge of nature, life, mind, universal truths, Yin and Yang, and of the Tao have all been incorporated by the Chinese in their study of complex human behavior in war-like situations. The principles in the book, Bing-Fa, through time have been incorporated into every facet of Chinese life. It touches modern Chinese society at all levels. But it is not just limited to China. The book is studied throughout Asian society.

Sun-Tzu's Bing-Fa is the most complete book of military strategy that has survived to the present. It consists of 13 rather short chapters. Chapter One is a summary. It gives an insight into the entire work and provides the basic strategy for the laying of plans. The principles outlined in this chapter can easily be generalized to apply to the world of business as well as military situations.

Sun Tzu stated that the art of war is of vital importance to the survival of a nation; a matter of life and death, a road either to glory or to ruin. The subject cannot be dealt with lightheartedly or with neglect. A battle should not be waged unless its strategy is carefully examined. Every battle determines the future of a nation and its people.

Marching into the 21st century, the military battle will likely be supplanted by the international economic battle for two major reasons. First, global society has generally recognized (with a few notable exceptions) that military solutions are impractical given the destructive capabilities of present day weapons and their far-reaching, residual effects that can return to haunt the perpetrators. Second, global economic interdependency and interconnectedness have made the control of a country possible without military force.

Harmony of the Five Elements

1. The Tao addresses the morality and righteousness of a battle: who is fighting and for what purpose.

This must be thoroughly understood by those who would affect the outcome. There must be a unity of purpose, not only among the leaders, but also among those led. In today's economic warfare the Japanese government and people have a strong commitment toward the success and survival of the Japanese race, the Japanese economy, and the nation of Japan. Since Japan is no longer a military state its survival is vitally connected to economic success. Japan has always understood this.

This is less evident in China. China has been unable, or less able, to unite its people and its government. One of the contributing factors is China's immense size. History has proven repeatedly that the Chinese people tend to be more bound to provincial concerns than to the greater good of China.

The people of Taiwan are more akin to the Japanese. When survival is difficult, the people unite. Taiwan is a very small island, whose only asset is its 19 million people. The survival of 19 million people hinges on Taiwan's economic success. Taiwan has created a unity that extends from the highest level of government to the most basic element of the country, the individual, and has been able to move toward economic growth with a unified purpose.

2. Heaven is signified by Yin and Yang, manifested as summer and winter and the changing of the four seasons.

One must understand nature's timing, and function accordingly. This has significance in economic dealings. Today, changes and unpredictable political situations dominate the economic environment. Complex foreign and domestic policies are ever changing, yet they function within this cycle of natural timing. With understanding, this can be used to one's benefit. It is important to know which cycle is coming to the fore at a given time. To know Heaven is to understand the timing of nature, the timing of uncontrollable elements. Understanding the nature of timing is knowledge of the soul. Even having a superficial understanding of these philosophical concepts will give you insight into the strategies of your Asian trading partner.

3. The Earth contains far and near, danger and ease, open ground and narrow passes.

These geographical features reflect matters of life and death in a military situation. The same is true in a business situation. The Earth is like a business entity. Geographical features are like business methods. The naturally occurring geographical features, either positive or negative, can be turned into resources that will enhance economic success and national survival. American business executives, when examining the the Chinese geographic-business method, do not detect the weaknesses of the Chinese. They often have not understood the cause for the inefficiency of their marketing efforts in foreign lands. Not until being beaten again and again did the West begin to examine the business methods of the East, and learn how to turn any situation to an advantage in this "Battle of International Trade." Let's look at Taiwan: a small island, two-thirds of which is mountainous. Most of Taiwan's population is located in the western coastal region. Taiwan decided to use its people, its main resource, to its best advantage. Taiwan's success in this endeavor is evidenced by the nation's progress. Taiwan, by providing a good educational system and encouraging a strong work ethic, has risen to become one of the economic giants in today's world. Japan and Korea have employed the same philosophy and have also made excellent use of their assets.

The United States, full of rich resources, high quality education, ingenious and creative people and scientific leaders, is envied by the comparatively disadvantaged Asian countries. To the degree the United States does not understand or effectively use these strengths, it has not realized its' greater potential; it is much like an army with advantageous terrain that does not exploit its position.

4. The commander must be wise, trustful, benevolent, courageous, and strict.

In Asian society, there is no difference between the qualities of a military commander or an industrial leader. Management requires the same characteristic qualities of wisdom, trust, sincerity, benevolence, courage, and strictness to carry out policies. These are the qualities that Asian society seeks in management personnel. If leaders lack these qualities, they will not receive the support of workers, which leads to low productivity and discontent.

In American companies there is often a great lack of empathy between management and workers. The workers tend to be loyal to the union and to labor in general. Often they have different objectives than management. Furthermore, significant differences in salary between management and workers add to the problems. In Japan and other Asian countries, these salary differences are much smaller. But the important thing in Japan is the commitment from all levels to the success of the enterprise, which is often sadly lacking in American industry.

5. Organization and discipline must be thoroughly understood.

Delegation of authority and areas of responsibility within a military or a business organization must be absolutely clear. Proper organization and discipline are the fullest expression of management's skill with the workers and their affairs, and have the greatest effect on results.

Americans tend to have less tightly managed organizations than do Japanese and, in some cases, this can mean lax discipline and even confusion. On the other hand, American companies encourage much greater individuality which, in turn, promotes innovative activity.

The degree of organization and discipline in Japanese companies gives the impression that they are running military camps. That impression may be increased by their insistence that everyone, including upper management, wear the same uniform. This innovation has been analyzed by certain management psychologists as creating a feeling of equality that facilitates communication vertically along the corporate pyramid. Management is accessible and they are perceived as working towards a common goal with labor, having different but equally important roles to play in the realization of that goal.

These five elements of The Art of War are of great importance to a successful operation. All five are intangible. They are not bigger guns, faster horses, more vehicles or more people, but intangible, spiritual, psychological elements. These fundamental rules not only will promote the success of a business operation, but the Commander-In-Chief of the United States should take them to heart when next he requests a larger budget for military hardware. If the Vietnam War taught one thing, it is that military hardware does not win a war; people, and people's commitment, do.

War, A Game of Deception

The most important concept in all Chinese military books is that the essence of successful warfare is deception. The objective of victory should be achieved through any means and to deceive the opponent plays a vital role in the strategy of war.

In line with this concept, if one is able and strong, then one should disguise oneself to be weak and inept. In 200 B.C., during the Han Dynasty, the first Emperor, Kao-Zu, had difficulties with the Northern barbarians. He led a march of 300,000 troops to the north. Kao-Zu sent a scout to investigate the barbarians' encampment in order to determine whether they were weak or strong so that he could plan his approach appropriately. The Northern barbarians hid their fat horses and strong soldiers so the scout saw only weak horses and tired soldiers. When the scout returned with his report, an advisor to Kao-Zu cautioned the Emperor. The advisor said when two countries declare war, it is usual to exaggerate an army's strength to intimidate the enemy. However, when one sees only weak horses and tired soldiers, it is probably done deliberately. The advisor felt surprises would be forthcoming and advised the Emperor not to attack. Kao-Zu did not listen. He took his soldiers northward and was surrounded by the barbarians for seven days, blocking supplies. The Emperor was later released through a peace talk strategy employed by one of his advisors.

In 611 B.C., the nation of Chu fought against Yung. The army of Chu was very capable in battle. Chu's advisors told the Emperor they should deceive Yung. They advised the Emperor to appear incapable of fighting Yung by deliberately letting Yung defeat them seven times. Yung came to believe the nation of Chu was not able to take a hard blow and grew arrogant and less security conscious. Chu later combined with other nations and destroyed Yung with great ease.

When you are ready to attack, you must express the idea that you will not attack.

In Chinese history this deception has been repeatedly used. In 800 B.C., during the Autumn-Spring period, Zheng wanted to attack his barbarian neighbor, Hu. He did this by marrying his daughter to the Emperor of Hu to express friendship. Zheng then told members of his court that he wished to exercise his military superiority and asked which country he should hit first. One of his advisors said the country of Hu should be first. The Emperor of Zheng expressed great anger and had the advisor beheaded. Zheng said, "Hu is my brother. How can we attack him?" The people of Hu heard of the event. They saw the Zheng emperor as sincere and no longer guarded against him. Later, Zheng made a dramatic military march on Hu and totally destroyed it.

When you are close, pretend you are far, but when you are very far, you must give the illusion that you are close.

This refers to temporal as well as spatial distance. If you plan to attack your enemy in the distant future, you must give them the illusion that you are going to attack immediately. The anticipation of attack will keep them on guard and constantly uneasy, thereby dissipating their resources. If, however, you wish to attack immediately, you must give the impression that you will not attack until a later time. This will cause the enemy to relax their guard.

In 205 B.C., a Han general set camp across the river from his enemy. His enemy thought the Han general would attempt to cross the river and prepared for him. The Han general pretended to prepare to cross the river for a decisive battle, but simultaneously sent 20,000 of his best soldiers up river to cross and go behind the enemy camp. He was successful and seized the Emperor of the enemy.

One Should Bait the Enemy With Small Gains

The basis of this strategy lies in human greed. The Chinese have always understood that the greatest assets China has are its one billion consumers and a vast land full of natural resources. These assets are an effective bait to foreigners competing in the Chinese marketplace.

An example of how the Chinese bait the West is to call for bids on a lucrative project. They then tell each bidder that their bid looks like it has a good chance to win but more information is needed; perhaps an education session arranged and paid for by the Western company. The result is the Western companies end up giving the Chinese free educational seminars. In the end, it may be that they change the specifications on the project, and accept only a company that is willing to enter into a joint venture with the Chinese; with the Chinese providing land and labor and the Western company providing finances and equipment. This is not meant to be an indictment of Chinese methods; rather, it is a word to the wise. The situation described can end up being quite profitable for the company that enters it with their eyes wide open and aware of the methods of Bing-Fa.

If the Enemy Is Well-Prepared, Strong, Well Trained and Secure In All Areas, Avoid a Direct Confrontation

The Chi attacked the nation of Lu. Lu's Emperor was ready to sound the drums for attack. The Emperor's assistants advised against it. The Emperor asked why and his assistants replied that, when the men are ready for battle and they hear the first drum, their spirits will be aroused with great courage. When they hear the drums a second time, their spirits are a little dampened. The third time the drums are sounded, their spirits will descend. Then when Chi's forces hit their drums three times, the spirit of Chi's soldiers will be low. That is when Lu should sound the first drum and march with high spirits. In such a way, the enemy's strength can be avoided and victory gained.

A small U.S. company can use this tactic to win a contract from away from a larger company by avoiding the strength of the large company. The Chinese like closeness and accountability which is easier to achieve when dealing with a small company. The Asians like to do business with friends that they can trust and a smaller company is, by design, more personal. Also a small company can present itself as an expert in a given field and therefore as having the ability to operate more efficiently and economically. A small company should avoid all direct confrontation when it comes to the sensitive subject of "size."

One Should Arouse An Opponent's Anger Creating Disorder, Causing the Opponent to Make Foolish Moves and Creating Opportunities

General Li Yuan conquered the Sui Dynasty and founded the Tang Dynasty. He attacked a city guarded by a great general of Sui. General Li's son told his father that, although the Sui general was brave, he lacked strategy. Li's son believed they would be able to trick him into coming out to battle. Li set up troops for ambush outside the walls while his two sons, with a few dozen soldiers, arrived at the city gates and threw abuses at the general in the city. The old general of Sui became very angry. Because of his temper, he opened up the city gate and came out for battle with 30,000 soldiers. He was ambushed and captured alive. This strategy was used on Andre Pierre when the Chinese picked apart his minor inconsistencies.

You Must Express Humbleness, Sincerity, and Weakness, Allowing Your Enemy to Grow Proud and Arrogant

The method used can be language, material, or many other things. The objective is to appear inferior and allow your opponents to grow superior and arrogant.

At the end of the Chin Dynasty, 200 B.C., there were two groups of barbarians. Eastern Hu was very strong. They sent an ambassador to Mouduen because they had heard Mouduen had a most precious horse which was considered a treasure of the country. The Ambassador said the King of Hu would like to have it. The King of Mouduen said that he felt one should live peacefully with neighbors and he gave the horse away. It was, after all, just a horse. Not much later, the Eastern Hu sent another ambassador. The Hu Ambassador told the King of Mouduen they had heard of the beauty of Mouduen's Queen and said that they wanted her. The members of the Court were furious. The King of Mouduen then stated a beautiful lady was a small price to pay for peace, and he sent his Queen to the neighboring nation. The Eastern Hu grew arrogant believing the Mouduen feared them because the King had expressed weakness. The Eastern Hu then asked the King of Mouduen for some of his land, as their own country was full of wasteland. The King of Mouduen then organized his troops and marched on Hu. Hu was not ready for such a confrontation believing by Mouduen's past actions that they were inferior and would never dare attack. Mouduen easily defeated them and regained all that was lost. This demonstrates the technique: "Use retreat as a form of attack."

When Your Opponent Is Inactive, Give Him No Rest

There was a rebellion during the Tang Dynasty. When rebels attacked, the Tang general would withdraw. When the rebels left, he chased them. During the day, he used drums to show off his military strength and at night he attacked giving his opponents no rest. After he made chase for several days he said, "Now the enemy is tired and we can strike." He easily destroyed the rebels.

This is a hallmark of the Chinese negotiating style: a long tiresome marathon which can go on for over a year, off and on, off and on. It has been proven to be effective against the West.

Sever the Enemy's Alliances, Leaving Him Totally Alone

This is a strategy the People's Republic of China has practiced with the Republic of China, Taiwan. The People's Republic has severed the alliances of the Taiwanese government. This has been done in a ruthless, inexorable way, like a lion hunter stalking a lion, never letting up. China has spent a great deal of time and has made use of every asset to isolate Taiwan's diplomatic position. This is unique in today's world. East and West Germany, for example, can participate together in many places, such as the Olympics. This cannot be done with China and Taiwan. This is a direct result of the programming the Chinese people have received for thousands of years. A method of controlling your opponent is to isolate him from the rest of the world. Here, it can be seen in action in the twentieth century.

Victory Is Determined Before the Battle Begins

A general, wishing to win a battle, must make a calculated plan. The loss of a battle can often be traced to inadequate calculations. Thorough calculation and planning lead to a victory, and insufficient planning and calculation lead to defeat. Defeat is guaranteed in the absence of plans. By examining the degree of planning, we can foretell the outcome of a battle.

The Five Essential Methods for Victory

There are five essential methods by which one can surely obtain victory.

1. One must know when to fight and when not to fight.

One who understands the nature of timing, and that there is a season for everything will react with forethought and dispassion instead of succumbing to and being defeated by his or her own emotions.

One must know when to match a large force with a small force. One who understands the rhythm of the battle and is able to freely utilize all of the natural advantages can realize victory with a smaller force or inferior position.

2. The one who has the total support of his troops will succeed.

One who understands how to obtain unconditional support by creating a common objective that is shared by all of his troops will have the advantage. Japan has made an art of moving their populace to contributing to the common good.

3. He who is well-prepared to seize favorable opportunities will win.

If one sharpens his intuition so as to detect the right timing and take appropriate actions, opportunities will be seen and seized.

4. He who possesses leadership and is free from interference from his sovereigns will succeed.

If an emperor is constantly giving orders to his general, his general cannot fight an effective battle. Freedom from such interference is essential. If a general has been chosen well, he should be given the freedom to win the battle.

5. When the victory is long-delayed, weapons will grow dull and morale will drop.

Before waging warfare, one must understand that victory depends on speedy action. It is costly to delay a battle, and long delays can drain the country's treasury. A delay also has an effect on the productivity and farming of the country. Weakening the country by waging a long war may give a neighboring country an opportunity to successfully invade.

As military strategies, some of these principles may have been rendered obsolete by technological advances, but as principles of negotiation, they are very valid. Looking back to the story in Chapter 1 of Andre Pierre, one advantage the Chinese had was time. As long as Andre Pierre was in China, he was trapped and his provisions had to be transported over a long distance. When a foreigner has to live in Beijing for an indefinite period, it is a very costly operation. For the foreigner, Beijing is one of the most expensive cities in the world. He must also cope with foreign food and culture, adding to his disadvantage. If the negotiations had taken place in Paris, I can assure you they would not have been long or exhausting. The Chinese understand the fundamental disadvantages of waging a long battle in a foreign land. Because of this, important negotiations rarely occur outside of China. The Chinese might come to visit a foreign company on a short-term basis, especially if the foreign company is willing to pay for the trip, but when it comes to bottom-line negotiations, the Chinese use the home court advantage.

On July 7, 1937, Japan declared war on China. Japan claimed they would conquer China in three months. The Japanese clearly understood that the only way to win in China would be to do so quickly. Just maintaining troops in China and holding onto captured areas was an expensive and exhausting undertaking for the Japanese. China understood its greatest asset was time. If China could keep fighting, it would ultimately win. Japan conquered Nanjin almost immediately, but China had secretly moved its capital far into the interior. China then continued to fight Japan for eight years.

According to the Chinese -- in something of an over-simplification -- five elements are involved in running a successful business project: (1) measurement, (2) cost, (3) forces, (4) balance of possibilities, and (5) victory.

One must first know how to measure the best time and distance. The military commander measures time and distance, and distance can become time. From a time, one can determine a cost. Once the cost is known, one can gather the forces to execute the project. By gathering the right working forces, one can balance the possibilities of success or failure. Then, one can prepare for victory and success. Once an understanding of these five elements is achieved, one can march to challenge the opponent. The alternative is not knowing effects of the five elements and only hoping for success.

The Highest Form Of Victory Is To Conquer By Strategy

In Chapter 3, under the title "Strategy", we read: "To win a battle by actually fighting is not the most desirable. To conquer the enemy without resorting to war, conquering the enemy by strategy, is the highest, most desirable form of generalship. The next best form of generalship is to conquer the enemy by alliance. The next is to conquer the enemy by battle on open ground. The worst form of generalship is to conquer the enemy by besieging walled cities. The besieging of walled cities should be avoided whenever it possible. Therefore, the most skilled in warfare are those who conquer the enemy without fighting battles, who capture cities without laying siege to them, and who annex states without prolonged warfare. They can preserve their forces whole and intact while struggling for the mastery of their opponent. They can win a complete victory without as much as wearying their men. All this is due to the use of strategy."

After World War II, the Japanese, partly from necessity and partly from design, took a good look at themselves, their past and particularly their future. They considered the principles set forth under Harmony of Five Elements in this chapter. The Japanese had, during World War II, used the worst form of generalship -- to conquer the enemy by battles and besieging walled cities. They literally ensured their defeat in the war when they won the first battle.

Now the Japanese have transferred their efforts to an arena that better suits their capabilities. They have achieved the understanding that "the marketplace is a battlefield" and they have converted that understanding to effective action. They have aligned their economic forces, led by a strong alliance among government, industry and the trading giants, and compete with America and the world on a level battlefield.

Japan is a walled city of regulations which prohibit the free flow of American goods into their market. When they meet with resistance from the American public due to the trade imbalance, they then apply the strategy of alliance by building manufacturing plants in the U.S.

A battle is fought by men, and the essence of a man is the human spirit. The essence of the human spirit includes his determination and emotion. The ultimate objective in conquering is to defeat the opponent's determination and emotion -- his spirit. The highest form of victory is to conquer by strategy, triumphing over the opponent's spirit, making the use of weapons unnecessary. The use of weapons to defeat the physical form ultimately defeats the spirit, but if one can subdue the spirit first, there is no need for laboring in expensive battles.

The Opportunity For Victory Is Provided By The Enemy

The Art of War, Chapter 4, "Tactics," says a force engaged in warfare can only make itself secure against defeat. It cannot be sure of the opportunity for victory. Such opportunity must be provided by the enemy. One can know victory, but one cannot assure or create a victory. This philosophy is based on Lao Tzu. Lao Tzu's philosophy is non-action; the fruits of action are a gift of the Tao. When an enemy provides the opportunity for victory, it is a gift from Heaven. One can prepare for victory and secure against defeat, but victory is provided by Heaven in the form of the enemy's miscalculation and ill-preparation.

Should the Japanese get all the credit for their economic success? I don't think so. The Americans have aided the Japanese in their victory by inadequate international trading policies and lack of effort in foreign markets. U.S. trade policy has been defensive; a successful effort in the foreign markets must of offensive. The U.S. seems particularly deficient in the spirit of offense in international trade.

Sun Tzu said, when one is skilled in the tactics of defense, he can hide beneath the Ninth Level of the Earth -- the deepest, darkest, most inaccessible place in the universe. When one is skilled at the tactics of offense, he can maneuver his force to an advantageous position above the Ninth Level of Heaven. Here, he can assure his safety as well as complete victory.

When a victory is seen by all, the victor deserves no praise. When a warrior succeeds in battle, the warrior deserves no praise. Lifting thin air is not an indication of one's strength. Seeing the sun and moon does not indicate sharp vision. Hearing thunder does not indicate superior hearing.

By the standard of the ancients, those who win with ease in a way unexpected by most men, as in the case of a superb commander, often do not receive praise for their wisdom or courage. Yet, they never fail to assure victory before they commence action. The superior commander secures victory before he battles. The defeated is one who challenges an enemy before he ensures success. The superior commander cultivates the Tao and strictly protects defense, law and order. It is then within his power to control the elements of success.

The Combination Of Direct And Indirect Maneuver

The Art of War, "Formation": All battles are the combination and use of direct attack and indirect maneuver. This combination results in infinite resources. In music, there are eight musical notes which, when combined, can produce an endless number of sweet melodies. There are three primary colors which can produce an infinite number of beautiful colors. There are five flavors detected by the tongue, yet combined, these produce numerous palatable sensations. In the same way, a limited number of tactical principles can be combined into an infinite number of strategies.

Order gives birth to chaos and disorder. Courage gives birth to fear. Strength gives birth to weakness. Order or disorder depends on the organization. Courage or fear depends on the manner in which advances are made. Strength or weakness depends on appearance.

This expresses the deep influence of Lao Tzu. Lao Tzu said we can see beauty in the universe because there is ugliness. We can see good because there is evil. Have and have not arise together. Difficulty and ease compliment each other. Short and long oppose each other. High and low balance each other. Music and sound harmonize with each other. Front and back follow one another. In essence, there is no difference between goodness and evil, between high and low, long and short, difficulty and ease. The basic elements motivating human beings, such as fear and courage, arise from the same place. They are two sides of the same coin. One can turn fear into courage, or courage into fear because they come from the same place in the essence of our being. One does not have to be fearful or courageous, strong or weak. One can be all things at all times depending on the circumstances. One can freely use all human elements for maximum advantage.

The indirect maneuver is so subtle, so small, it is seemingly formless. It is mysterious and soundless. Therefore, one is able to hold the destiny of the enemy.

Use of Local Guides

The Art of War, Chapter 7, "Military Maneuvers." If one does not use local guides, he will not be able to count on natural advantages. This is true in today's foreign trade. It is very important to use local guides, experts on that particular country or in that particular field, to take full advantage of the circumstances. The Chinese distrust and feel distanced from foreigners. They feel at ease with other Chinese whom they consider to have a loyalty to the motherland. All Chinese are the children of Ian Di and Huang Di and share the same values and understanding. This trust extends to Chinese living overseas, because Chinese are never bound by passport and nationalities, but by race and common ancestors. This is true with the Japanese and Koreans as well.

A guide interprets the outcome of meetings, considers subtle hints, verbal and nonverbal actions and reactions. He aids in sorting out the negotiating team to determine who is the top man and how the decision-making process is being carried out. The guide, or interpreter, can establish very important informal channels of private communication. The guide should have an understanding of American business practices as well as Chinese business practices, culture, and socio-political structures. He should be able to quickly gather and analyze information on each negotiator's background and determine what the individual profit centers are. He should provide the proper interpretation of the progress of the meetings and the direction things are going.

Keep Plans As Dark And Impenetrable As Night; Move Like A Thunderbolt

This is a description of Chinese negotiation, especially if the foreigner does not have the advantage of someone expert in Chinese language and culture. During negotiation, the plans of the Chinese become darker and full of surprise elements which can create frustration for the foreigner engaging in negotiations without expert help, like the Frenchman in Chapter 1 who experienced so many difficulties because he was totally in the dark. After nine months of negotiation, to have the signed agreement subsequently declared invalid struck him like a thunderbolt.

Attack When the Opponent is Least Prepared and Least Expects It

This is a common notion. America has fallen into the trap, however. An early end to the Korean war was in sight in October, 1950, when American troops were marching towards the Yalu River at the Chinese border. On Thanksgiving Day, over half a million Chinese troops crossed the border. The Americans allowed the holiday spirit and festivities to affect normal preparedness, so they were relaxed. China's selection of Thanksgiving Day to make a massive attack on the U.N. forces was not an accident; rather, it was a calculated choice.

These methods of deception are the essence of military victory. It must be determined when to use each strategy.

An appropriate decision must incorporate the peculiarities of each situation.

Lao Tzu says, in his Tao Te Ching, "One who is skilled in walking leaves no track. One who is skilled in speaking makes no slip. A good reckoner needs no tally. A good door needs no lock, yet cannot be opened. A good binding requires no knots, yet cannot be loosened." Following this train of thought, a good plan is dark and impenetrable. It gives no direction of movement. If it moves, it does so like a thunderbolt, with no previous warning.

Although the Westerner has had his share of experience with surprise and deep subterfuge down through the centuries, the English and American tradition of openness and fair play tend to make those Westerners naive and vulnerable to Chinese-style deceptions. The Westerner comprehends the possibilities, of course (Hitler, for one showed the way), but his tradition and psychology is such that he can't quite bring his expectations to the necessary level. He does not quite believe it could happen. Thus, the Japanese success at Pearl Harbor. In reality, instead of trustworthiness and honor, the Chinese sometimes offer surprise and deception. There are deeper mysteries with the Chinese mind. (This does not mean, that the Chinese are without honor, but the distinctions and difficulties are deep and hard for the Western mind to grasp.)

The Art of War, "Army Mobilization." When the enemy's messenger is humble in manner and speech and his troops are simultaneously increasing in number, they are about to attack. When the enemy's messenger is arrogant in manner and speech and the troops movements appear hasty, they are about to retreat. When the enemy speaks peace, this indicates the plotting of deception.

Asians analyze their opponent's every move to the smallest detail, including the manner of a messenger. The Chinese mind is trained to interpret every move to determine intent in order to totally understand his opponent. The Westerner, confronted with the Asian scrutiny, sends off signals he is not aware of, and which can create additional difficulties for him.

Japan's present economic strength makes it a dominant influence in the world economy. But Japanese messengers, even the Prime Minister, seek to appear submissive to American politicians. The Japanese pretend to be less than they really are. The Americans, on the other hand, may assume a superior position over the Japanese, even when borrowing money. When a messenger is humble and submissive, advancement is the true intention. Japan is making economic advances while appearing submissive.

Some American journalists and politicians are taken in by Asians and the posture of Asians. They become believers and are diverted from their own objectives. In Asia, humility is a weapon as well as a virtue.

From The Art of War, "Order the army to act, but do not inform them of your plan. Show the army the advantages, but not the possible dangers."

The current Japan-U.S. relationship can be used as an illustration. Japanese politicians often make promises to U.S. politicians, knowing full well the promises cannot be fulfilled. They show the U.S. the possible gains and tell them what Japan is going to do to solve the trade imbalance, but they never disclose the full plan and their true intention. They only show the possible gains, but not the future problems. Just think about it. What will happen if Japan buys out all of our real estate and our factories in the United States?

When Facing Death, the Struggle For Survival Will Give New Birth

It is perhaps a simple truth but when an army finds itself in a desperate situation, it will struggle for survival. When an army is facing extinction, the struggle for survival will give birth to new ideas, new actions. Thus, when an army is completely trapped and in great danger, the imagination and boldness inspired by the crisis may turn defeat into victory.

The recent history of Japan provides an example. The Japanese understand the value of Chinese Bing-Fa and are often the better practitioners. Following World War II, the Japanese nation faced death. This death gave birth to a national determination not to see death face-to-face again. The Japanese have always believed the survival of the Japanese Imperial race takes precedence over any other cause. Even fundamental individual survival ranks below the Japanese objective of survival as a race.

The fact that Japan is an island country occupied by a largely homogeneous people tends to inspire a greater commitment to survival. Through application of this strategy, Japan has rebounded to become the international economic leader and a lender to the U.S. government.

Something similar happened to Taiwan. When the government of The Republic of China, lead by Chiang Kai-Shek, retreated from mainland China in 1949, the fate of what remained of the Republic of China was at its lowest and most bleak period -- faced with an empty treasury, defeated troops, hordes of refugees, gathered in this island of approximately 36,000 square kilometers, and living daily with the threat of a military invasion from mainland China. Now, 39 years later, the Republic of China has established itself as one of the world's foremost economic forces, with annual import/exports reaching 88 billion U.S. dollars and foreign currency reserves in excess of 76 billion U.S. dollars.

Use of Spies

The Art of War, "Espionage: Use of Spies." An army may be forced to fight for years, yet victory may be decided in one day. If a leader is unwilling to pay a thousand pieces of gold to employ spies, he will remain ignorant of his enemy's condition. This is extremely inconsiderate to his own people. Such a man cannot be a good leader. He cannot be a useful assistant to his sovereign if he is unable to master victory. To obtain information one cannot depend on gods and spirits, nor just inductive or deductive calculation. One must obtain information from those who have a thorough knowledge of the enemy's condition.

The characteristics of one who uses spies are detailed in this chapter. In ancient China, it was considered that the person able to use the right spies to do the right thing and subsequently interpret the information gathered was of a certain character. Besides the presently well-known qualities of subtlety and ingenuity being necessary to use the information obtained through espionage, it was considered that only the wise and holy could successfully use spies; only the benevolent and righteous would find the right men for espionage and would use clear and correct judgment in handling them.

This is less understandable to the Western mind and somewhat hard to convey with just the right nuance. It also seems to put spies, and the head of a Chinese espionage organization on a higher plane than, say, the head of the CIA and his men.

It was clear that the use of spies was regarded as vitally important. The ultimate goal, then as now, was to obtain information to gain a thorough understanding of enemy conditions. But to achieve the best possible utilization, the information needs to be analyzed and interpreted by a man of real discernment, inner strength and character, clear in the heart, wise in the mind, benevolent towards himself and mankind. Only such a man will have the ability to interpret gathered information and put it to use.

This is difficult in today's world. In business, military, and political maneuvers, individual egos can often interfere with the ability to judge and use information properly. An inability to select the right person to gather inside information or an inability to understand and interpret the gathered information can be a disadvantage for Westerners in dealings with the East.

In California's Silicon Valley, the high tech center of the world, many Japanese companies have offices among hundreds of U.S. companies. The American engineers often joke about the Japanese companies being "spy stations." It is not a joke to the Japanese.

This chapter also gives a complete definition of the five types of spies. The local spies use the enemy's local people to gather information. The inside spies bribe the enemy's officials to gather information. The converted spies, or counterspies, use enemy spies to provide information and return propaganda to the enemy. Doomed spies are those who enter into a situation knowing death is the only way to get their information out. The missionary spies enter the enemy camp and return with information. The manipulation of each type of spy was totally worked out in ancient China. The Art of War emphasizes that it is most important to reward spies with the highest rewards because spies can save one from untold losses in treasure, lives, and territory.

In Chinese philosophy, a leader must rule in harmony with Tao. By being attuned to the essence of creation, Tao, all things are revealed to him. This leads to a proper perspective on the information provided to him, whether or not it is covert. The Oriental mind is disingenuous. It does not take things for granted. To understand the use of spies is the most mysterious display of a leader's ability.

In today's complex business world, gathering and interpreting information about one's competitors requires the same ingenuity used in spy operations in ancient China. Sun Tzu said, "Know yourself, know your opponents, one hundred battles, one hundred victories". This is the essence of The Art of War, and the application of its methods are the only hope we have of developing a proper strategy in our interaction with Asia.

7 THICK FACE - BLACK HEART: THE ANCIENT CHINESE SUCCESS SECRET

Thick Face - Black Heart

The lust for power has been the single most important influence on the destiny of Chinese empires. It has resulted in the succession of dynasties. Sons have killed fathers and brothers have set their swords against brothers in the quest for power. The allure of domination kept China in a state of constant war for hundreds of years. One such war lasted from 755 A.D. to 1080 A.D. During this period, China's population dropped by 37%; from 52,910,000 to 33,300,000 - a loss of almost twenty million people, a startling figure, considering this war was waged with spears and arrows.

The battlefield is now the board room and the suits of armor have been replaced by Brooks Brothers suits, but the lust for power has not changed. Each individual, whether political leader or businessperson, seeks power in his own way, according to his environment. If the goal is reaching a business agreement with foreigners power is realized by obtaining the most favorable business terms.

In Chinese thinking, winning or losing depends on how the score is kept. A Westerner may view a business transaction as satisfactory from their side, while, at the same time, the Chinese may term the same result a victory for China.

"Mutual benefit" has become a popular term in reference to dealings with the Chinese. They clearly understand that their natural resources are like the pot of gold at the end of the rainbow to the foreigners. They watch the long line of foreign traders at their door waiting to do business with them and realize they have the advantage.

When a foreigner completes the extensive and troublesome paperwork necessary to visit China, he feels grateful just to have the chance to present his case. Regardless of whether or not he ever completes a business transaction with the Chinese, the Chinese feel half of his benefits are already realized simply by the fact of his company having the opportunity to market in China.

They also expect that another one-quarter of these foreigner's "benefits" will be voluntarily forfeited in the spirit of friendship, demonstrating the foreign company's desire to help in China's modernization. The Chinese believe that the rich Western companies should be benevolent and lend them a helping hand because China is poor. They believe that, under the principles of humanity, some of the Westerner's profits should be given up to maintain their newly established friendship.

From the Chinese point of view, the lion's share of the benefits to which foreigners are entitled should be non-monetary. They believe the monetary benefits should be left to the Chinese. If this seems outrageous, perhaps this excerpt from Lucian Pye's book, Chinese Commercial Negotiation Style, can help explain: "For various reasons, the Chinese feel that the world sees them as somehow 'special,' giving rise to a peculiar revival of the traditional Middle Kingdom complex, which leads Chinese to expect special consideration and treatment." After the 13th Congress in 1987, there was a strong emphasis on China's commitment to the path of modernization. As a result of this, China, at the higher levels of the central government, began to acknowledge the need to protect the foreign companies' interests. However, newspaper slogans are one thing, reality, quite another. The foreigner will still need to fight every inch of the way to insure the profits to which he is entitled.

The Chinese negotiator must obtain the best possible terms for any deal he makes. If he does not, the consequences may be dreadful to his company and his career. There is only one employer in China. The qualities they deem essential for successfully conducting business are known to the Chinese as "Thick Face and Black Heart."

In 1911, The Chengdu City Daily ran the first installment of an article entitled "Hou Hei Xue," by S. W. Lee (Thick Black Theory). The article was to be published in three installments, but the controversy created by the first installment was so overwhelming that the remaining installments were never published.

A friend of Mr. Lee's in Beijing published a booklet entitled: Thick Face, Black Heart, which included all three sections of the article. The book was published several times between 1934 and 1936. Each edition sold out immediately despite the controversial and somewhat negative image of the Chinese people that it portrayed. The original article was scarcely 2000 words long, yet its effect has been far-reaching. The book was banned in Taiwan almost 20 years ago and is still not available today in China.

The book was both successful and controversial because the Chinese who read it knew that what Mr. Lee said was true. But, the majority of the people were not ready to acknowledge the unvarnished truth. The people with the most to lose, those in power, forbade the reading of the book, calling it "evil influential material." The book endured, however, because the Chinese recognized the material as truly representative of beliefs held by most Chinese. Mr. Lee had written of events which often motivate the Chinese individual's daily life.

"Thick face, black heart" is a term used to describe the "must have" quality of Chinese political and business leaders. Mr. Lee illustrated his theory with examples from Chinese history. His intention was to diagnose "thick face, black heart" as a sociological disease. Acknowledging the existence of a disease, he felt, is fifty percent of the cure.

The concept of thick face, black heart is very simple and its execution very effective. When used in small matters, small rewards are received; when used in larger matters, larger rewards are received.

God gave each one a face, with the thickness within. God gave each one a heart, with the blackness within. The face and heart are not great in size, but if carefully examined, the thickness within the face has no boundary and the blackness within the heart knows no end. In this world, greed for material gains and desire for fame and power to control and manipulate others all come from this mysterious place.

The concept of a "black heart" is easy for a Westerner to understand, while a "thick face" might be a bit more obscure. Recall, as described in Chapter 4, the importance of "saving face." Then consider the Western idea of a person having a "thick skin"; in other words, a person who does not care what others think. So, a person with a "thick face" is not bound by the conventional thinking of others and thereby can achieve things unachievable by someone worried about the appearance of his actions to others. The only concern this person has about his actions is whether or not they are effective.

For thousands of years, there have been different schools of thought regarding human nature in China. First, it is believed that man is born with a pure tendency and nature. Evil is added after birth by the environment and other influences. Another school teaches that man is born with evil tendencies and he must struggle his whole life to remove the evil within. Yet another school teaches that man is pure in his natural state because he is created in the image of the divine and has all the divine qualities. But, because of the power of maya (creative delusive power), evil is created within the heart. So the quest of each human lifetime is to remove the veils of delusion and to express the divinity within.

Whether or not one accepts any of these propositions, it seems obvious that blackness does exist in the heart and is activated by human emotions such as greed, jealousy, hatred, anger and fear. These emotions manipulate humans like a puppet's strings. Move the right string and the puppet will move accordingly. Although there are a few extraordinary people who have the ability to control their mind and emotions, each one of us can recall being a victim of our own black hearts.

There are three stages to thick face, black heart:

The first stage: Thick as a castle wall and black as charcoal.

At first, the face is paper thin. Then it grows from inches to a foot, from a foot to many feet. In the beginning, the heart is white as ivory. Then it becomes gray. Gray turns into blue, and eventually the heart becomes black as charcoal. Although the castle wall is thick, the cannon can still destroy it. And charcoal is black and unattractive. People do not want to get close to it.

When you achieve this stage, you have mastered only the beginner's skill.

The second stage: Thick and hard, black and shimmering.

Those who achieve this stage of thickness cannot be moved or disturbed by any humiliation. Those who achieve this stage of blackness feel like a blackboard; the darker they get, the more desirable they feel darkness to be. The second stage is superior to the first, but the thickness and darkness are still visible for all to see.

The third stage: So thick it is formless; so black it is colorless.

The highest and most difficult level to achieve is when it becomes so thick and black it transcends form and color. For example, in Buddhism, one must see the tree beyond its form, until there is no longer a tree. Then, you have truly mastered the knowledge. In stage three, then, one must master formlessness and colorlessness.

Lee said, "Thick is such that the more you polish, the thicker it gets. Black is such that the more you wash, the blacker it gets. Like calluses on the hands and feet, the more you rub, the thicker they get."

Thick and black lie naturally within human nature. When a child is born, his face is thin. The more the child is abused by the world, the thicker his face becomes. Those with black hearts   may try to cover them with virtue, so the blackness will not show through, just as a bitter pill is coated with sugar. But when the sugar coating is washed off, the blackness will reappear.

Mr. Lee went on to say that there are two kinds of actions. The first you may act on but not talk about. The second you may talk about but not act upon. These two behaviors are acceptable to our common moral standard. For example, one may do anything the heart desires in the act of making love, but to speak of it in public is unacceptable. Two friends may curse each other's mothers, as long as the curses are only spoken but never acted upon.

Although the principles of thick face, black heart may never be mentioned in today's Chinese business and political world, they will certainly be acted upon. It is considered that to use them for self gain is a lowly deed. To use them for the good of all is a virtuous deed. When dealing with foreigners, the practice is used for the good of one's country and, therefore, is a noble action.

Lao Tzu said:

The Tao of Heaven is like the bending of a bow.
The high is lowered,
And the low is raised.
If the stick is too long,
It is shortened.
If it is not enough, then it is made longer.
The Tao of Heaven is to take from those
who have too much,
and given to those who have none.
Man's way is different.
He robs the poor for the rich.

In the Three Kingdom period, Cao Cao's success secret was black heart. He killed anyone in his way of gaining power. He said, "Its better to wrong others then to let others wrong me." Cao Cao's counterpart, Liu Bei, had an extremely thick face. Whenever he was otherwise unable to get his way, he would resort shamelessly to tears in front of the other party and would thereby change a disadvantageous situation to his favor. Throughout history, many have commented that Liu Bei's country was obtained as the direct result of his tears. Chinese history is full of respectable heroes who either had thick face or black heart or sometimes both.

Taking Care Of Business Chinese Style

In Mr. S. W. Lee's collection of writings, Mr. Lee relates two ways of taking care of business often seen in Chinese society. One is to "saw off the arrow" and the other is to "patch up the wok." Although these methods are not subscribed to by all Chinese, their use is common enough that they bear mentioning.

Saw Off the Arrow

A man is hit with an arrow and goes to see a doctor of surgical practice. In China, surgical practice is called Outer Practice and internal clinical practice is called Inner Practice. The surgical practice doctor, to whom the man has first gone, saws off the arrow's shaft but does not remove the arrowhead. He tells the patient that the job is done. The patient asks the doctor, "Why don't you remove the arrowhead inside my body?" and the doctor replies, "That is a job for the Inner Practice doctor." The Chinese often take care business by the "saw off the arrow" method. If one is presenting or suggesting something to be done, he may often hear: "Regarding this matter, I really agree with you, however, I must discuss this with Mr. Chen." In this example, Mr. Chen serves as the internal doctor. You may often hear: "I will take care of a portion of the job, leaving the rest for later." This is believed to be an effective way to defer accountability. Sawing off the arrow can avert many problems considered unnecessary by the Chinese, but it causes major delays in political and commercial negotiations requiring commitments.

Patch Up the Wok

The household wok has a crack causing a leak so the owner summons a wok craftsman to repair it. The repairman looks at the wok and begins to scrape off the accumulated grime on the bottom of it. (In old China people used coal as fuel causing the bottom of the wok to accumulate a lot of grime.) The craftsman tells the owner to start a fire so he can burn off the grime. When the owner goes off to start the fire, the craftsman quickly uses his hammer to hit the wok lightly, enlarging the crack. When the owner returns, the craftsman shows the wok to the owner, saying, "The crack on your wok is longer than it first appeared. Now that I have scraped off the grease, you can see the entire thing. I will patch it now." The owner looks at the wok carefully and replies with great surprise: "You are right, you are right! If you had not discovered the problem today, I would probably have been unable to repair this wok at a later date." So the craftsman repairs the wok and everyone is happy.

Hitting the wok is an art. If it is hit too softly, the crack will not increase. If it is hit too hard, the crack will become too large for repair. If the wok is made of clay, the whole thing might break into pieces.

We often witness "saw off the arrow" and "patch the wok" being used together. The possibilities are endless with these two formulas. I will leave it to the reader to contemplate them.

Expectations

The Chinese understand that Americans expect everyone in the world to treat them equally, like the way they treat the rest of the world. The Chinese use this to maximize their potential benefits.

When Chinese look at Americans, two things enter their minds. One, the Chinese envy the material comforts so readily available to the American, which are beyond their realistically achievable dreams. The other is distrust.

As a result of events in the last two hundred years, Westerners represent humiliation and defeat to the Chinese people. The Chinese believe that the Westerner should pay for the privilege of dealing with them. "Since the Westerner has more, he should pay more." This also derives from subconscious historic influences. Since the West has robbed the kingdom of China without conscience so many times in the past, it is okay to rob them back. This is demonstrated often in business arrangements between China and the West, where overcharging for material and labor to a Western partner is a standard practice.

Liu Bang's Weapon

After the end of the Chin Dynasty, from 207 B.C. to 202 B.C., Liu Bang and Xiang Yu battled for control of China. Xiang Yu had everything going for him: he had the best troops; he already controlled most of China, and he had great personal ability as a warrior. Yet, he lost China to Liu Bang. Contributing to his final failure were his inability to listen to his highest ranking advisor, and not acting with as thick a face as Liu Bang. Liu Bang repeatedly lost battles and returned home for new recruits. When Xiang Yu lost only one important battle, he felt so full of shame that, instead of returning to his homeland to regroup and recruit, he chose to take his own life.

When we compare black hearts, Xiang Yu was not in the same class as Liu Bang. When Xiang Yu captured Liu Bang, he was planning to kill him during a banquet but, at the last moment, Liu Bang's adviser skillfully appealed to Xiang Yu's reason as to why it was inappropriate to kill

Liu Bang and, therefore, gave Liu Bang the opportunity to escape.

Years afterwards, Liu Bang and Xiang Yu met on the battlefield. Xiang Yu was unable to conquer Liu Bang's force. Xiang Yu had been holding Liu Bang's father as hostage for years. So, Xiang Yu ordered Liu Bang's father be brought out and tied in front of a pot of boiling oil ready to be cooked unless Liu Bang retreated with his force. Liu rode to the front of his troops and shouted out, "You and I were blood brothers one time, therefore, my father is also your father. If you wish to cook your father, please share a cup of the broth with me." This story amply demonstrates the blackness of Liu Bang's heart. Mr. Lee illustrates above that, because Liu Bang was a skillful practitioner of the Thick Face - Black Heart theory, this led directly to his success in conquering and uniting China.

It is easy to understand why Mr. Lee's thesis has caused both consternation and controversy within the Chinese scholarly community.

36 STRATEGIES

A Chinese person once asked me, "Do the foreigners (Westerners) also have things such as the 36 strategies?" I replied that I believed Westerners do use similar strategies but they were not so conscious of doing so and do not dedicate their entire life to mastering a set of precise techniques.

36 Strategies is a book that deals with methods of deception in all daily encounters. The origin and the author of this work are unknown. It is an historical book 1,500 years old, composed of 36 sections that describe the refined principles behind these Chinese strategies. The expression "36 strategies" is a common phrase used by the Chinese people to describe someone's actions as

deceitful. Even Chinese children are aware of this meaning. The Chinese often say that their study of these strategies is not motivated by a desire to learn how to deceive others, but rather to recognize and prevent these strategies from being used against them.

The original text of 36 Strategies often uses words and expressions related to the I-Ching (The Book of Changes). China's greatest military strategists such as Sun Wu, Sun Bin, Han Xin, and Li Chin were all well versed in the I-Ching and utilized the theory of "I" (Change) in military philosophy and strategy. The 36 Strategies, using the I-Ching's principle of ever-changing Yin and Yang, describes methods to manipulate specific manifestations of this duality: active and inactive, soft and strong, direct and indirect, conventional and unconventional, real and false, attack and defense, labor and rest, guest and host, you and me, superior and inferior, empty and full, arrogance and humility.

Strategy 1 - Deceive the Sky and Cross the Ocean

This is a method where, to accomplish one's objective, a falsehood is openly displayed and the truth is hidden. An opponent's attention is thereby focused on the false situation, allowing the true objective to be easily accomplished without detection. This is much like the distraction a magician creates to lead his audience's attention away from his sleight-of-hand.

To illustrate, I remember a movie starring Audrey Hepburn. Her husband had hidden a million dollars before he died and everyone was looking for it. Although her life was in great danger, she simply did not know where the money was hidden. It turned out that it was in her purse, visible all the time, glued to a letter: a set of used stamps, each of which were worth several hundred thousand dollars.

The following is an historical illustration of the use of this technique. This incident occurred during the end of Southern and Northern Dynasties which were comprised of nine countries and lasted from 420 to 589 A.D.

The vision of the Sui was a united China. In 589 A.D., Sui attempted to conquer the country of Chen. Sui's general maneuvered his troops back and forth along the Yangtze River. After each movement, they made an encampment in the Anhui province directly across the river from Chen, displaying a great array of banners and many tents. In the beginning, Chen thought Sui would attack soon, so they gathered all their military strength to prepare for defense. But, after these maneuvers were repeated many times, Chen concluded the troops were merely Sui defensive troops engaged in routine military exercises and felt great relief. Chen's defensive forces relaxed and Sui seized the opportunity to attack and defeat Chen. The Sui Dynasty was established in 589 A.D. and China was united once again, bringing to an end nearly 300 hundred years of division.

Another illustration occurred during the Spring-Autumn period (770-476 B.C.). Two princes, Xiao Bai and Jiao, escaped from the country of Chi to avoid assassination by their brother, the newly established ruler. The two princes had advisors named Guan Zueng and Bao Su who were best of friends. They vowed to assist their respective princes in different neighboring countries and to wait for the right moment to overthrow the despotic ruler. Guan and Bao promised each other that no matter which of their princes then succeeded to the throne, one would assist the other to rule the country.

Prince Xiao Bai managed to be crowned king and sought to have his brother's advisor, Guan Zueng, returned to him from the country of Lu where he was living in exile. If Lu knew his true intention, which was to have Guan Zueng become Prime Minister and assist him in ruling the country of Chi, Guan Zueng would never have been released. In order not to create any suspicion in Lu, Xiao Bai downplayed the situation by requesting that Guan Zueng be returned as a prisoner for punishment, offering to exchange for Guan Zueng a bounty of a mere five lamb skins. To further display to Lu that he really did not care about Guan Zueng, he sent a common jail cart to transport the prisoner back to Chi. Prince Xiao Bai fooled Lu by treating the exchange of Guan Zueng as he would a transaction involving an ordinary prisoner.

Parenthetically, at this period in China, the country was divided into small feudal kingdoms that were continually seeking ways to conquer the others. Every king sought superior strategists and advisers and, as mentioned earlier, the "Eating Guest" was very popular in this period.

Guan Zueng proved to be one of China's most clever strategists. At this time, China was often attacked by the Northern barbarians who constituted a great threat to the survival of Chinese civilization. With the assistance of Guan Zueng, Chi became strong and united all of the feudal lords to battle the barbarians and provide law and order in China. Confucius said that, without Guan Zueng, Chinese civilization would have dissolved.

Conclusion: If we see a situation as a usual event, it arouses no suspicion. The darkest of secrets are often hidden in the open. From the Chinese view, Yin exists in the Yang, Yang exists in the Yin; light in darkness, darkness in light.

Strategy 2 - Surrounding Wei to Rescue Zao

In 354 B.C., the period of the Warring States, the country of Zao was under siege by the country of Wei. Zao requested assistance from the country of Chi. Chi sent General Tian as commander and China's great military genius, Sun Bin, as military strategist. General Tian wanted to charge the capital of Zao and battle with Wei, but Sun Bin disagreed. Sun suggested, "All the strong troops of Wei are presently in Zao, so this causes the interior of Wei to be empty. If we attack Wei's capital, the army will naturally return to Wei to defend its own land." General Tien accepted the strategy and marched toward Wei. As soon as Wei heard Chi was attacking Wei's capital, the troops immediately turned around to go back to Wei. Chi's army had already set a trap for Wei. They destroyed Wei's army, releasing Zao from danger, as well as gaining an easy victory over Wei.

Conclusion: Instead of taking a strong enemy head-on, one should divert the enemy's strength, attack vital points, and avoid direct confrontation. This will achieve the desired result with much less effort. Sun Tzu's Art of War (Chapter 6): When attacks are aimed directly towards an enemy's weak points, the advance becomes irresistible. In Sun Bin's Art of War (Chapter 2): There is a conversation between King Chi and Sun Bin. The King asks, "Is there a strategy that can use one to attack ten?" Sun Bin replied, "Yes. Attack the enemy's weak point; attack the enemy where he least expects it."

Strategy 3 - Borrow Another's Hand to Kill

This is a method used to fight without dirtying one's own hands. To protect one's interests, one may utilize a third party's position to create a contradiction which results in the elimination of the enemy by the third party. This has been employed in Chinese social and political life since the beginning of China. In order to use a third party to accomplish the task, one must create a cause for confrontation in the mind of the third party.

In the Warring States, King Zu had a Prime Minister, Nang, and three assistants. Among the three assistants, Fei was very jealous of his brother assistant, Buo, because he was the king's favorite. One day Fei went to Prime Minister Nang and told him that Buo requested he attend a party at Buo's home. Prime Minister Nang graciously accepted the invitation. Fei then went to Buo's house and informed him that the Prime Minister was coming to dine. Of course, Buo had no reason to refuse. Fei asked Buo what kind of gift he would prepare for the Prime Minister.

(In China, it is imperative, when one is visited by distinguished guests, that a gift is given to express pleasure at their acceptance of the invitation.) Buo could not think of an appropriate gift. Fei reminded him of the Prime Minister's love of weapons and suggested that Buo choose from the arms recently captured from the country of Wu. Fei told Buo to arrange the arms inside the gate so that when the Prime Minister entered, Buo could ask him to inspect the arms and could present them to him. When the day of the party arrived, Fei went to the Prime Minister's house in great distress. He told the Prime Minister not to attend the party because there were armed soldiers in Buo's house waiting for his arrival. The Prime Minister did not believe this so he sent his confidant to examine the situation. The confidant came back and verified there were arms ready at the gate. In great anger, the Prime Minister arrested Buo. Buo realized he had been set up, so he took his own life.

Another story in the Spring and Autumn Annals tells of King Zhang. He wanted to attack the country of Kuei. Before he marched to attack, he ordered a list prepared of all the most capable people who served the King of Kuei. He then made a public announcement, accompanied by the sacrifice of animals (a common practice of the times) and priests offering prayers to Heaven. King Zhang stated that, upon the conquering of Kuei, he would divide the land among those capable individuals. Heaven and Earth were to be his witness. When the King of Kuei heard about this, he thought he had been betrayed by his advisors, that they had all been bought by King Zhang. King Kuei was moved by great anger so he killed all of them. Kuei was then left without the benefit of wise advisors and King Zhang conquered him with ease.

Conclusion: When uncertain of one's own position, one may utilize the force of a third party to eliminate obstacles. Sun Tzu's <u>Art of War</u> (Chapter 6): When destiny is subtle and formless, intangible and mysterious, the strong-minded one is able to hold the fortunes of the enemy in his hands by creating the third element to insure the desired outcome.

Strategy 4 - Make Your Enemy Work While You Wait at Leisure

If you are in an inferior position, in combat with a larger enemy, drag and delay. The enemy will tire, forcing him to lose his sharp, enthusiastic spirit. All the while, you rest and wait for the right time.

This strategy is a basic element of current Chinese negotiating techniques. The story of Andre Pierre is a typical example. The French, Americans, Italians or Germans start with a disadvantage in their dealings with China by having to travel a long distance to be in China for negotiation. When the great expenses involved and the prolonged agony of less-than-perfect living conditions are combined with culture and language differences and government red-tape, one is exhausted after two weeks of negotiation. A month later, one is homesick and sick of China, while the Chinese are fresh and ready to do battle. Prolonged negotiations make the final contract much sweeter for the Chinese. I have never seen the Chinese go to the Western world to negotiate a business venture using this delaying tactic. In the case of Andre Pierre, I am surprised he kept his sanity as long as he did.

Conclusion: While the enemy's position is strong, one should not attack directly, one must utilize elements of the situation to cause him to grow tired and thus change from strong to weak. As the Chinese aphorism states, "There are only 24 hours in the day. If the day is long, the night must be short." If the night can be made longer, then the day will become shorter. If one can cause an enemy's position to worsen when one's own position remains unchanged, one moves from an inferior to a superior position. Sun-Tzu's __Art of War__ (Chapter 6): Those who arrive on the battlefield early will have time to be rested as they wait for the enemy. Those who arrive late rush into battle when they are already exhausted. The one who is skilled in warfare forces the enemy to encounter hardship in coming to him while he waits in ease.

Strategy 5 - Use the Opportunity of Fire to Rob Others

When someone's house is on fire, use this chaotic situation to steal their possessions. Use someone else's misfortune for self gain. There are two kinds of fire. The first is arson (created by one who wishes to rob another), where the opportunity for easy advantage is inherent. The second is the fire that is started by unknown or accidental causes and one merely takes advantage of it. In old China, when a neighboring country was in distress from natural calamities such as flood or drought, this situation was interpreted metaphorically as the second, or accidental, type of fire. This offered the perfect situation for attacking a weakened foe with a greatly enhanced possibility of conquering.

There is a very popular story about the overthrow of the Ming Dynasty (1368 - 1644 A.D.). The bandit Li's superior army had entered Beijing's Forbidden Palace after his army had swept almost the whole of China. The defense force was demolished and the Emperor had hung himself from a plum tree on the back hill of the palace. Li had declared himself the Emperor of China.

As General Wu, stationed at Shanhaiguan (the most eastern part of the great wall), was preparing to surrender, he heard that his most beloved concubine, Chen Yun Yun, had been captured by the bandit, Li. In his fury and thirst for revenge, he turned to the Northeastern Manchurian people for help. The Manchurian were the barbarian neighbors of China and were considered the subjects of the Chinese Emperor. They were often mistreated by the Ming court. Manchuria, like a hungry tiger, had been long awaiting this opportunity. General Wu, leading the Manchurian army, charged into China and in just a few short days, Li was destroyed. This brought about the end of the Ming dynasty and established the Ching dynasty with the Manchurian, Nur Ha Tseh, as Emperor. The Manchurians took advantage of the "fire" in China to enter China to help put out the fire and to stay as conquerors.

Conclusion: Victory is gained by benefiting from the misfortunes of your opponent. Sun Tzu's <u>Art of War</u>

(Chapter 1): When the enemy is thrown into disorder, crush him.

Strategy 6 - Display in the East and Attack the West

Disguise the direction of your troop movements by diverting the enemy's attention to the east when your intention is to attack in the west. Since this has been done repeatedly throughout Chinese history, unless it is most cleverly applied, the results could well be unsatisfactory. The most important element of this deception is to understand the enemy's reaction to a given situation and then to out-guess him. Sometimes this strategy needs to be combined with other methods in order to deceive the enemy.

At the end of the Han dynasty and the beginning of the Three Kingdoms (198 A.D.), Cao Cao attacked the Southern city of Nanyong. Commander Zhang of Nanyong was forced to retreat behind the city wall and prepared to defend it to the death. Cao Cao circled the city for three days. He discovered the wall at the Southeastern corner was constructed of a combination of new and old stones. Cao Cao knew from his experience with the construction of fortifications that this meant the Southeastern corner would be the weaker part of the city wall. As a ruse, he gathered all of his troops at the Northwestern corner to display signs of attack. Commander Zhang's adviser had been watching Cao Cao circling the wall and was also aware that the weakest point of his defense was the Southeastern corner. Knowing the strategic ability of Cao Cao, he was certain that Cao Cao had discovered this weakness and was setting a trap. Commander Zhang decided to accommodate Cao Cao's strategy. Zhang ordered all of his soldiers to exchange clothing with the civilians and sent the civilians to the Northwestern corner to prepare for its defense. Meanwhile, all the professional soldiers hid in the Southeastern corner waiting for the attack. Cao Cao's troops secretly entered the Southeastern corner at night. He was defeated by Zhang's awaiting army. So, Cao Cao used this strategy, but Zhang saw through his deception and countered with his own application of the strategy.

Conclusion: The objective of this strategy is to camouflage the focus of intended activities, although it is not often so simple as to feint at one corner of a wall when one's real objective is the opposite corner. It is often so difficult for a Westerner to see any direction or purpose at all to Chinese negotiations that the Chinese negotiators achieve this strategy without too much effort. In Western military strategy, this method has also often been applied. The most notable example was the World War II landing of allied troops in Normandy after manufacturing evidence so convincing that Hitler and the German High Command were fooled into believing that the attack was to come far to the north.

Strategy 7 - Create Something from Nothing

If there is no wind, there are no waves. Wind must be created if waves are desired. It is more difficult to create wind than to create events that allow one to manipulate a situation to one's advantage. In order to create favorable events or situations, one need only find a buyer for the mental images created and, when there is a clever, willing seller, there is usually no shortage of willing buyers.

In China, it is believed the Emperor is the Son of God and that it is destiny for a certain individual to become Emperor. If power is seized through a revolution and a Dynasty overthrown, it is considered the will of Heaven. In China's history, there have been two peasants who led revolutions and overthrew the existing dynasties. These men founded the Han (206 B.C.-220 A.D.) and the Ming (1368-1644 A.D.) dynasties. Liu Bang, the founder of the Han dynasty, was a small county official during the Chin dynasty. The first emperor of the Ming Dynasty had at different times been both a beggar and a monk. They both successfully convinced the people that they were the true Son of God by convincing them that their special unseen auras were the symbol of God. When one can create deception according to the symbols that are acceptable to one's historical period, there is an excellent possibility that one will succeed. The aura of the Son of God obviously could not work today, but the principle remains.

This following example is from the book, The Three Kingdoms. During the Three Kingdom period, in 208 A.D., at Chibi in Hubei province, Cao Cao and the General of Wu were facing each other across the Yangtze River. Cao Cao, who was controlling the puppet emperor, was preparing to invade Wu. Cao Cao's army outnumbered the Wu forces by more than ten to one. Besides an extreme shortage of troops, Wu also lacked weapons and had an extremely small supply of arrows. To remedy the situation, the night before battle a small contingent from the army of Wu sailed halfway across the river in ships covered with straw. The soldiers shot a few arrows from the straw-covered ships into Cao Cao's camp. Cao Cao's army returned the fire with a hail of arrows. Wu's Commander General then turned his ships 180 degrees and received another volley from Cao Cao's camp. When the ships were loaded with several hundred thousand arrows, the Wu Commander General shouted to Cao Cao, "Thanks for the arrows," and the ships retreated. This strategy of "something from nothing," by getting many arrows by such a ruse, helped Wu's army to eventually defeat Cao Cao's army. Today, Japanese business people are studying The Three Kingdoms, and regard it as one of the best books on strategy and deception in the literature of China.

Another illustration is drawn from the Tang dynasty period. In 755 A.D., An Lu San rose against the Emperor and surrounded a city in Henan Province. An Lu San's forces outside the city's wall were superior in number to the Emperor's forces, but the Commander of the City, Zhang Xuen, decided to defend his city to the last man. Zhang Xuen ordered the making of many thousands of straw men. The straw men were dressed like soldiers and lowered over the city walls by rope. Outside the city walls, An Lu San's soldiers thought the straw men were real soldiers preparing to attack and they shot at them. Like the straw boats, Commander Zhang's straw men received hundreds of thousands of arrows. Zhang later ordered five hundred real solders to be lowered over the city walls. This time, An Lu San's soldiers did not shoot because they thought that it was another ploy to make them waste arrows. They laughed and ignored the whole thing. Zhang

Xuen's five hundred real soldiers then charged into the enemy camp, surprising and defeating them.

During the Korean war, the opposing forces often faced each other from fixed positions for long periods of time. The Chinese used empty cans to make noises at night to disturb the Americans. At first the Americans got nervous and stayed very alert, but after many nights of this, the American soldiers became accustomed to the noise and relaxed. The Chinese then attacked unexpectedly.

Conclusion: The objective of this strategy is to make the unreal seem real; the empty, full. According to Sun Tzu's Art of War (Chapter 6), the good warrior imposes his will on the enemy, but he does not allow the enemy to impose his will on him.

Strategy 8 - Secretly Utilize the Chen Chang Passage

During the battle between Liu Bang and Xiang Yu, at the end of the Chin dynasty (208 B.C.), Liu Bang was forced to retreat to the Sichuan province. Liu Bang wanted to allay Xiang Yu's suspicions of immediate counter-attack, so he destroyed the only road to Sichuan province. Later, when Liu Bang was ready to march back into central China, he openly began to repair the destroyed road. This led Xiang Yu to believe Liu would not be attacking him until he finished the road. Instead, Liu used the previously unknown Chen Chang passage and took Xiang Yu by total surprise, thus defeating him and establishing the Han dynasty.

This strategy has been utilized in different ways. During the Three Kingdom period (220-265 A.D.), the country of Wu was persuaded by the country Su to enter jointly into a battle against Cao Cao. For strategic reasons, the army of Su occupied Jienzhou, an important city of Wu, during the battle. After they had defeated Cao Cao, Su refused to remove their troops from Jienzhou. General Lu of Wu accepted the responsibility for recovering Jienzhou. Knowing Wu wanted to retake Jienzhou, Su set up a great defense system headed by the famous General Kuan. Lu feigned illness and assigned a young man named Sun to take over his duties. Kuan's arrogance rose when he saw that an inexperienced young commander was assigned to retake the city. Sun posed no threat so he moved his troops northward to engage Cao Cao in further battle. Lu then returned and seized the opportunity to sail up the river to Jienzhou. Having disguised his battle ship as a merchant, Lu sailed up the river to the city docks unchallenged and retook Jienzhou.

Conclusion: Mastering the use of "open and secret," and "truthfulness and deceit," results in victory. In Sun Tzu's Art of War (Chapter 11), one should vary his plans according to the situation of the enemy in order to obtain victory. In the beginning, when enticing the enemy to battle, one may appear to be as shy as a young maiden. Then, when the enemy shows an opening, one must move as fast as a fleeing hare and catch the enemy by surprise. According to Sun Tzu's Art of War (Chapter 1), one should attack the enemy where he is least prepared and when he is least expecting it; and one must feign weakness to make the enemy grow arrogant.

Strategy 10 - Knife Hidden Under the Smiling Face

This strategy is used to gain an advantage over an opponent by inspiring trust in him so that he lets down his guard. Military action is then taken when trust is instilled.

The Chinese do not necessarily limit themselves to a single strategy. Often, several strategies are combined. Recall the story of General Kuan, who grew arrogant when he saw the young, inexperienced General Sun stepping in for General Lu during Lu's supposed illness. General Sun furthered the deception by sending a letter to General Kuan confessing that he had always been a great admirer of General Kuan and wished to seek peace between the two countries. Sun compared Kuan to many legendary military leaders and professed that he (Sun) was merely an incapable scholar full of admiration for General Kuan's ability. Sun did this to insure that General Kuan would dismiss him as no threat and would then direct his attention northward to Cao Cao.

In the meantime, the country of Wu secretly negotiated a peace agreement with Cao Cao to avoid having an enemy on either flank. (Cao Cao to the north and General Kuan to the west). General Sun used the Knife Hidden Under the Smiling Face in the form of a letter, while the leaders of Wu negotiated peace with Northern enemies so they could concentrate their efforts on their Western enemies. General Kuan was deceived by this strategy and lost the city of Jienshou when he moved his troops northward. Later, he was captured by Wu in battle and beheaded.

In modern history, the Japanese attack on Pearl Harbor serves as an example of this tactic. Japan prepared for years to attack the United States, while Japanese diplomats used every means at their disposal to assure the United States that they wished to maintain peace. They wanted the U.S. to be totally unprepared for attack. Negotiations continued right up until December 7, 1941, when Japan wiped off the smiling face and revealed a hidden knife.

Conclusion: Today, this strategy is used more for economic warfare than for military gains. Beware of smiling faces and the banner of friendship.

Strategy 11 - Plum Tree Sacrifices for the Peach Tree

There was a plum tree with a peach tree growing next to it. Insects came to attack the root system of the peach tree. The plum tree volunteered to take the place of the peach tree and sacrifice itself to the insects. This teaches that the whole is more important than any of the parts. In order to accomplish the objectives of the whole, parts must at times be sacrificed.

Remember the story of Sun Bin's three horses. He won the match by sacrificing the chance of his worst horse winning by matching it against his opponent's best horse. Sun Bin then put his best horse up against his opponent's middle horse, and his middle horse raced the opponent's worst horse. Sun Bin won the match, two victories to one.

Some time later, Sun Bin marched towards Wei's capital while the army of Wei was fighting elsewhere. The Wei commander ordered his troops to return to defend the capital in three groups of unequal strength. Chi's commander wished to use the strategy of the three horses against Wei's three armies but Sun Bing did not. He said the objective here was not to have two wins, but rather to destroy the greatest number of enemy troops. Sun Bin then divided Chi's troops into three, using his weakest force to fight the enemy's strongest, the middle force was sent to fight Wei's middle force, and the strongest group sent to fight the weakest. The first two groups needed to pick their ground carefully to be able to prolong the battle. Chi's strong group quickly destroyed the enemy's weak force, and joined the middle force to create a superior power, rapidly defeating Wei's middle force. These two groups then joined to assist the weakest group which had been holding off the strongest of Wei's army and thereby gained total victory.

These two stories demonstrate an ingenious ability to identify the goals and objectives of each encounter and manipulate them according to the needs of the given situation.

Conclusion: In the business world, always keep the primary objective in sight and make adjustments according to each situation. Sacrificing parts can, in the long run, benefit the whole. Depending on the character of an opponent, one can set the bait accordingly. This is the principle of giving the insignificant and in return gaining what is significant.

Strategy 12 - Walk The Sheep Home, Just Because it is There

If you see a sheep beside the road without anyone tending it, take the sheep home and make it yours. This means that when you come across the opportunity for a small advantage, you should act upon it swiftly, turning the carelessness of your enemy to your benefit.

Remember the battle between Liu Bang and Xiang Yu. During this time, when Liu Bang was secretly using the Chen Chang passage to re-enter central China, Xiang Yu was busy conquering a rebellious lord in the territory of Chi. When Liu Bang emerged from the Chen Chang passage, he discovered three territories of the old Chin empire totally unguarded. Liu Bang took these territories as his own while Xiang Yu was fighting the Chi lord. Xiang Yu lost three territories in the west simply because Liu Bang happened to be there and claimed them as his own.

Recall the earlier story of the general who invited the Northeastern Manchurian people into China. From the Manchurian's viewpoint, they merely took advantage of an enemy and profited from their vulnerability. In this case, the untended sheep was China.

Conclusion: This strategy of turning one man's disadvantage into another man's advantage is used frequently in today's business world. Sun Tzu's Art of War

(Chapter 4), "The opportunity for victory is provided to you by the enemy."

Strategy 13 - Disturb the Snake by Hitting the Grass

To disturb the snake by hitting the grass can be, according to circumstances, either a desirable or an undesirable action. When the intention is to catch the snake by surprise, disturbing the grass would be a mistake. If, however, a direct confrontation is wanted with the snake, then hitting the grass is recommended so that the snake will make itself visible.

Most often it is better to refrain from disturbing the snake so that one can gain the advantage of surprise. When one knows the snake is in the grass, there is considerable advantage so long as the snake is not aware that it has been discovered. When one knows the enemy's intent, it may be best to feign ignorance. The enemy will not become suspicious if he believes his intent is not known. When it is to your advantage to flush the snake, hit the grass. See how the situation develops and work it to your advantage.

For the next example, we look back to the Three Kingdom Period. Cao Cao lost the battle at Chibi and retreated northward with a handful of troops. In the meantime, the Lord of Su refused to return the city of Jeinshou which he had annexed. General Zhou from Wu was furious over this. He set a trap for Liu Bei, baiting it with the promise of marriage to a princess of Wu. Liu Bei's advisors and strategists knew Zhou was simply setting a trap and that Liu Bei would not be allowed to marry the princess. They knew the proposed marriage was merely a ploy to lure Liu Bei to the country of Wu for capture. The strategists advised pretending they did not know General Zhou's intent. They instructed Liu Bei to send one of his best generals to the country of Wu with five hundred soldiers in his company. When the soldiers arrived in Wu, they dressed in festive clothing and took to the streets. They spread the news that Liu Bei was coming with rich gifts to marry the princess. Soon, the entire country was aware of the betrothal and the alliance between the countries of Su and Wu which it implied. This made it impossible to back off from the wedding plans and and so they gave the princess in marriage to Lui Bei. Lui Bei could not have married the princess of Wu if he had "disturbed the snake." The trap had been set and by feigning ignorance, Liu Bei worked the situation to his advantage.

Conclusion: Do not hit the grass disturbing the snake before carrying off the untended sheep, or before hiding the knife under a smile, or before crossing the ocean under the sky, or before taking the Chin Chang passage. Sun Tzu's <u>Art of War</u> (Chapter 7) states, that the best strategy to overcome an enemy is to stand as still as a forest on a windless day, to be as immobile as a mountain, to be as impenetrable as darkness.

Strategy 14 - Borrow Another's Body to Return the Soul

In Chinese mythology Li was a meditation master. One day, he told one of his students that he would be traveling in spirit to visit Heaven and that he would be back in seven days. The student promised to guard Li's body during those seven days and to look after it with great care. On the sixth day following Li's departure, the student received an urgent request to come home because his mother was gravely ill. The student wanted to see his mother again before she died. Li had been gone for six days, and the student wondered if he might remain in Heaven, never returning to reclaim his body. So, the student burned Li's body and left. Li returned on the seventh day. He was unable to find his body so his soul entered the body of a beggar who had just died on the roadside, thus giving the beggar's corpse new life.

Following Cao Cao's defeat in 211 A.D. at Chibi, he moved his army westward. Cao Cao attacked in Shaanxi province where over 100,000 troops belonging to different lords combined to defend the province against him. Cao Cao overcame them, nonetheless, and continued to move westward. Liu Zhang, the lord stationed at the city now known as Cheng Du in Sichuan province, was fearful of the advancing Cao Cao. He needed help, so he sent a messenger to speak to Liu Bei. At this time, Liu Bei was in command of tens of thousands of soldiers, but he had no base of operations. The messenger brought Liu Bei the chance he was waiting for. Liu Bei quickly gathered his troops and marched to Sichuan province. He later called the province his own. Cheng Du was a city without defense like a corpse without a soul. Liu Bei used the defenseless, dying city and gave it new life.

When a Chinese company is on the very brink of failure, occasionally through some stroke of luck, it may run into an uninformed Western company which will enter into a joint venture with the dying company. Thus, new life may be breathed into it.

Conclusion: A troop facing defeat in the battlefield may find a new situation and turn its defeat to victory. In today's business world, a company facing bankruptcy can find a new life through a merger. When one is facing the end of the line, a calm and clear head can often find a new body to borrow and return to business anew.

Strategy 15 - Entice The Tiger To Leave The Mountain

The tiger is powerful only when it is in its native environment -- the mountain. An effective means for controlling a dangerous and powerful person would be to entice him from his own environment; remove him from his power base.

When the CEO of a large U.S. company visits China on a business venture, it is like the tiger leaving the mountain. He leaves behind his impressive office building, factories, and his luxury car, replacing them with a hotel room, a taxicab, and the handful of people traveling with him. He is left struggling with a foreign language and the customs of a foreign land.

When Liu Bei wanted to enter Sichuan province during the Three Kingdom period, he gave the order to his generals. Liu Bei desired a speedy entrance to the province. Liu Bei's brother, Zhang Fei, was one of Liu

Bei's generals. Zhang Fei marched towards Sichuan province with 10,000 soldiers. When he approached the city of Ba Juan, Zhang Fei went to the top of a nearby hill and looked at the city. He saw that the the city of Ba Juan would be very difficult to seize by force. The only way to conquer the city would be to provoke battle outside the city walls. The problem was how to lure the commander of Ba Juan, General Yan, into bringing his forces outside the city gate.

Zhang Fei tried many strategies to entice General Yan out of the city. But Yan was an experienced general and he recognized Zhang Fei's trickery. Zhang Fei sent small groups of troops to camp outside the city gates and throw abuses at the old general. They tried to make him angry enough to come out and fight. Like Zhang Fei's other tricks, General Yan saw through the plan and made no move.

Finally, Zhang Fei sent scouts into the wilderness surrounding the city to seek an alternate route around the fortress. General Yan's spies discovered Zhang Fei's intention. They told General Yan which night Zhang 's troops would be leaving and the old general came out of the city to give chase. But Zhang Fei was prepared for General Yan. He disguised a common soldier in his own uniform and sent him with a small number of troops to the decoy route around the city. As General Yan chased the small group, Zang Fei came right behind and captured the old general.

Zhang Fei understood that he had to entice the tiger to leave the mountain. His genius came into play with the strategies he used to accomplish this. different strategies work, depending on individual temperaments. There are no absolute rules. The opponent's temperament must be understood and a strategy designed for each situation.

Conclusion: To deal with a person who is in an advantageous situation, one must alter the situation by removing the supportive elements. Examine the source of power, and if the source is an individual, remove that individual. If an individual's source of power comes from his strategist, then remove the strategist. Entice the tiger to leave the mountain. The key here is entice. It may not be easy to entice a wary tiger from the mountain. The nature of the tiger must be understood so that appropriate bait can be used.

Strategy 16 - In Order To Capture, One Must Let Loose

The original text tells us that if the enemy has no place left to run, his courage will rise. The enemy should be given room to escape, allowing him to tire physically and lower his morale. Like troops with no orders, the enemy will be totally defeated mentally. When not so much as an ounce of resolution can be found, then he can be captured. This will make for passive prisoners,and achieve a victory with less bloodshed.

The Prime Minister of Su, during the time of Three Kingdoms, was Zhu Ge Liang. While Zhu Ge Liang was battling with Eastern and Northern neighboring countries, his barbarian neighbor to the south repeatedly attacked Su, so Zhu Ge Liang decided to conquer his Southern neighbor. During the ensuing battle, Zhu Ge Liang captured the Southern chief and let him go. This drama was repeated seven times. Seven times the Southern chief was captured by Zhu Ge Liang and seven times released. Finally, the Southern chief swore total loyalty to Zhu Ge Liang. Zhu Ge Liang knew that to have real peace on his Southern border, he needed to have this loyalty demonstrated as an example to the remaining barbarians to the south. Without total peace in the south, Zhu Ge Liang would have been unable to deal with his enemies to the east and north.

Another illustration: Liu Bei, on his death bed, asked his Prime Minister, Zhu Ge Liang, to support and help his son. Liu appealed to Zhu Ge Liang to prepare his son as his successor if he could, but if Zhu Ge Liang felt Liu Bei's son was not suitable to be a future emperor of China, than Zhu Ge Liang should assume the position as Liu Bei's successor. Zhu Ge Liang, very moved by Liu Bei's request, did everything in his power to fulfill it.

This was the wisdom of Liu Bei. He knew if he gave room to Zhu Ge Liang to make his own choice about helping Liu Bei's son, he would give his life in the endeavor. Liu Bei's son did not have the power to become emperor without Zhu Ge Liang's assistance, and Liu Bei knew this. Liu Bei also realized that Zhu Ge Liang could take over as successor if he wished. Zhu Ge Liang did not need Liu Bei's permission to do so. Liu Bei, on his death bed, played a mental game with Zhu Ge Liang. He captured Zhu Ge Liang's heart by giving him the choice.

Conclusion: This strategy demonstrates a softer approach, showing the kinder part of human nature. The results, however, are most effective. In office politics of today, instead of severely punishing an erring employee, a dose of compassion and a light punishment might result in a more loyal staff.

Sun Tzu's <u>Art of War</u> (Chapter 7), says when you surround an enemy, you must leave an outlet for him to go free. Do not press a desperate enemy too hard.

Strategy 17 - Bait a Piece of Jade with Brick

Exchanging a worthless brick for a valuable piece of jade would be a great gain. But how do you get someone to give you jade when you have handed them brick? Again, an understanding of an opponent's character is essential. The bait must be tempting enough to the opponent for him to react. This strategy has been used over and over in today's international trade. The Chinese understand how to create bait for the Western enterprises.

The opening of China, following nearly forty years of isolation, is one of the most significant historical events of the late Twentieth Century. China has a population that stands at one billion, twenty percent of the world's population, plus immeasurable natural resources and a large expanse of land. The very name of China is representative of the ancient and mysterious. It is prestigious for a Western politician or businessman to be associated with China.

Western companies do not always do well in China. It seems that, when the Chinese hand out a piece of brick camouflaged as jade, the Western companies fall for the illusion. The game can be turned around, though, and handed back to the Chinese. One should enter the game fully aware that the camouflaged piece is brick, not jade. Pretend to be fooled and accept the brick in exchange for your jade piece. However, the jade piece you offer should have a hidden hook and ultimately lead to the attainment of your goals and objectives.

U.S. government officials often go to China to negotiate trade regulations or restrictions. Here, the Chinese have the upper hand. They know the U.S. officials feel they must accomplish the signing of some agreement while they are in China so they can look good when they return to the United States. The U.S. government official often feels that a signature on a disadvantageous agreement is better than none at all. Because the West needs to justify the existence of its bureaucracy, it tends to do something, anything, to show it is moving ahead. The Chinese bureaucracy has the opposite philosophy: doing nothing is better then doing something if there is the least possibility of being in error.

Each year, many Asian countries send purchase delegations to the United States. These delegations visit many states to make their purchases. The act of purchasing is a camouflaged brick. The jade they are looking for is political favor which will result in more favorable trade regulations or even improved diplomatic relationships. There is nothing wrong with this. The U.S. benefits from the purchases. But caution should be exercised to ensure that the jade piece given away will not be of too high a price.

Conclusion: It is important to understand the principles of human nature and personal gains. Often public approval can cloud the judgment and one can become a victim of this strategy. A person should recognize when this strategy is being applied and turn it to an advantage.

Strategy 18 - Defeat the Enemy by Capturing Their Chief

Defeat through capture of the enemy's chief is a principle everyone can understand. Throughout history, there are thousands of proofs of this strategy. But how can this be applied in the arena of international trade?

The real source of power, the decision maker, the chief, must first be identified, then conquered. A thorough understanding of exactly what the chief is looking for is required, then one must satisfy that need. If you cannot provide what the chief wants, you will not be able to accomplish the act of "capture."

In a socialist or communist country, identifying and satisfying the chief's need is much more complicated than in a capitalistic society. The chief's ultimate goal may not always be money. It may be his desire to obtain personal power in the party or bureaucratic system.

Conclusion: If the key to overcoming the enemy is to capture the enemy's chief, then how to capture this chief becomes the determinant for any successful venture. The knowledge of how to capture is dependent upon the ability to understand every facet of the chief. Sun Tzu's <u>Art of War</u> says, (which we repeat because it cannot be stressed too much); "Know yourself, know your opponents; one hundred battles, one hundred victories."

Strategy 19 - Remove the Firewood Under the Cooking Pot

The strength of the fire determines whether the water will boil. The strength of the fire comes from the burning wood. If the force of the boiling water is great and dangerous, one may not wish to directly confront it. By removing the firewood from under the cooking pot, one can cool the water and make the task easy.

In the Warring State period (476-221 B.C.), General Le defeated more than 70 cities of Chi. Chi was left with only two cities, one of which was Ju, commanded by Tian Dan. Tian Dan realized the source of the enemy's fierceness was General Le, so his first order of action was to remove the general. To this aim, Tian Dan planted the rumor that the general was dragging his feet in conquering the two remaining cities because he was planning to establish himself as the King of Chi. When this news reached King Yan, he immediately replaced General Le. With the formidable General Le out of the way, Tian Dan was able not only to defeat the army besieging his city, but to go on and liberate the 70 cities Le had captured.

Conclusion: Do not confront your opponent's strong points. Rather, avoid the strong points and remove the source of its support, thereby diminishing your opponent's strength. Use the direct and indirect, soft and strong combination of strategies to remove the source of strength.

In today's political and business negotiations, a person that plays the role of the firewood may take the form of a disagreeable individual that continually stirs up unnecessary difficulties and makes waves. Just as you thought everything was wrapped up, he adds more wood to get the water boiling again. More satisfactory results will be obtained for both parties by the removal or discrediting of this individual.

Strategy 20 - Watch the Fire Burning Across the River

A good strategist understands the optimum time for action or inaction. Acting at an inopportune moment can create poor results, just as poor results can come from not acting at the most opportune moment. Not pressing an advantage can give an enemy a chance to recoup his strength. But, when an enemy has conflicts within, an attack can become a common unifying force. Without this force, inner conflicts may surface and power struggles result. This is when it is best to watch from across the river for the most suitable time to make a move. Internal struggles weaken the enemy's inner strength and make for an easy victory.

Children in China know the story of the clam and oyster. A clam took hold of an oyster on the beach. The oyster retaliated by opening its shell and grabbing hold of the clam. The two hung onto each other, neither willing to give up its position. A fisherman happened upon the clam and oyster and caught them for dinner. The fisherman was able to effortlessly capture both because they were each unwilling to let loose of the other. The clam and oyster were in a poor defensive posture because of their own internal conflict and death came to them both by the hand of a third party.

The great General Yuan of Northern China died in 203 A.D., leaving his position to the youngest of his three sons. The elder brothers were displeased that the younger brother inherited their father's position and military power. Cao Cao attacked soon thereafter, and the three Yuan brothers united for battle. Cao Cao was unable to overcome the three in light of their union. On the advice of one of his strategists, Cao Cao left the area and returned south to battle with Liu Bei. This gave the Yuan brothers leisure time and so the conflicts the brothers had among themselves surfaced.

Just as Cao Cao had hoped, the three Yuan brothers fought with one another. The eldest brother was unable to overcome the younger two brothers, so he sent a messenger to Cao Cao asking for his assistance. Cao Cao accepted and sent his troops northward. Cao Cao killed the eldest Yuan brother and destroyed the troops of the two younger brothers. Cao Cao had allowed the three brothers to create their own fire and Cao Cao waited for the right moment to take action.

Cao Cao applied this strategy again against the two younger brothers. Following their defeat at the hands of Cao Cao, the two brothers escaped north to Laodong with several thousand of their troops. Cao Cao did not give chase. He knew the Lord of Laodong had always been afraid of General Yuan, and had fostered a deep hatred for the Yaun family. Cao Cao knew also that the Lord of Laodong would accept the two brothers with their troops because he feared an attack by Cao Cao. When no attack ensued, the Lord of Laodong relaxed and saw no further reason to give the two Yuan brothers sanctuary. Just as Cao Cao predicted, messengers from Laodong brought Cao Cao the heads of the two brothers a few days later.

In the case of the Yuan brothers, Cao Cao twice watched the fire burning across the river. By allowing the situation to develop on its own, a fire was created and Cao Cao benefited without using force and energy to fight a hard battle. It is important to know when to watch the fire and when to take advantage of it. Timing is all important.

Conclusion: Sun Tzu's <u>Art of War</u> (Chapter 4) says, when one is skillful in warfare, he must first place himself in an invincible position and then seize any favorable opportunity to defeat the enemy. To secure oneself against defeat depends on one's own efforts, while the opportunity for victory must be afforded by the enemy. Watching the fire burning across the river is the act of exercising the proper patience that allows events to progress until the situation is favorable.

Strategy 24 - Steal the Dragon and Replace with the Phoenix

Replacing the dragon with the phoenix leaves a totally different animal. Manipulating circumstances can change the inner dynamics of a situation favorably. Chinese history contains countless stories about this. They are kept alive in the mind of the Chinese people by passing them from one generation to another.

During the Sung Dynasty, Emperor Zhen Zhoung (who reigned from 997 A.D. to 1022 A.D.) had a beloved concubine who threatened the position of the Empress by giving birth to a prince. The Empress paid the doctor who delivered the baby to switch the baby prince with a dead fox. The Empress then took the newborn prince and claimed she had given birth to the baby boy. Because the concubine had apparently given birth to a fox, she was branded a witch. The concubine was sent from the palace and the Empress secured her position by becoming the mother of the next Emperor. The degree to which man can manipulate is limited only by the imagination, the thickness of face and blackness of heart.

The great wall was built by Chin First Emperor, who united China and established the Chin Dynasty. While he was out inspecting troops, Emperor Chin fell ill. He immediately wrote a will and named Crown Prince Fu Su heir and gave the royal seal to the Prime Minister, Li Si. After Emperor Chin died, Li Si feared that, because of China's instability, fights would ensue for the Emperor's throne. He kept quiet until he returned to the capital. Prince Fu Su was not notified of the contents of Emperor Chin's will. When Li Si reached the court, Eunuch Zhou Gou came to see the Prime Minister and asked, "Between you and Mr. You, who is closer to Prince Fu Su? I think that when prince Fu Su becomes Emperor, he will use You as Prime Minister and at that time your life will be in danger. I suggest you change the will, condemning Prince Fu Su to death and making Prince Hu the heir, in order to save your own skin." Li was confused and fearful after he thought it over and decided to follow Zhou's advice. He ordered Prince Fu Su to drink poison and Prince Hu became Emperor. Emperor Hu named his mentor, Eunuch Zhou, as Prime Minister and later Zhou killed Li Si and You.

Conclusion: The above cases are common occurrences in Chinese history. These principles are still being used in today's complex world of political and military covert operations, as well as in trade practices and human relationships.

Strategy 26 - The Hidden Message

The Chinese use this strategy often during daily life. They do not say things directly. Rather, they give hints by discussing a situation related to A while the message is really intended for B. This is a common tactic among the Chinese, and I have witnessed Chinese doing this with an American diplomat. The American did not understand the message. Often, when criticism is directed at A, the real target is B. It is a way of saying what needs to be said without provoking a confrontation. This strategy can be very effective in a sensitive situation if employed tactfully.

In a story from the Spring-Autumn Annals, Mr. You was in the favor of King Chu. One day, Mr. You met the son of the late Prime Minister, Sun, who was collecting firewood. Mr. You realized King Chu was not taking proper care of Sun's family. Mr. You entered the Court dressed like the late Prime Minister. This pleased King Chu who said, "Even the false one pleases me. I certainly miss Sun and because you dress and act like him, I would like to appoint you as the new Prime Minister." Mr. You told King Chu that he would like to discuss the matter with his wife. The next day, Mr. You told the King that he could not accept the post of Prime Minister. He explained that Sun had been the Prime Minister but now that he was dead, his son was so poor that he needed to go to the mountains to collect firewood. Mr. You said that his wife knew about this and felt that if he became the Prime Minister, she would share that same fate and starve to death. King Chu realized then that he had been remiss in not caring for the late Prime Minister Sun's family and rectified the situation by providing them with a generous pension.

Conclusion: An indirect statement is often considered the most important when dealing with the Chinese and other Asian peoples. One must listen carefully. The dropping of hints is a Chinese national pastime. If you miss a hint, it could turn out to be very costly in a business transaction.

Strategy 27 - Pretend to be a Pig in Order to Eat the Tiger

When a hunter goes to the mountain to hunt the tiger, he can bait the tiger by dressing as a pig. The unsuspecting tiger will not recognize the danger, thinking he is getting a pig for dinner. When the tiger draws near, he can be killed. When a strong enemy appears, pretend to be weak and display a smiling face to lower the enemy's guard. Wait until the right moment to move in to claim total victory.

In the period of the Spring and Autumn Annals, the country of Wu was very strong. Wu invaded the country of Yue and captured Yue's king and enslaved him and his wife. They were made to clean the cow and horse refuse and engage in other demeaning labor. They slept in a stone jailhouse. The King of Yue served the King of Wu with great loyalty. When Wu's king fell ill, the court physician said the only way he would live was to have someone eat his feces. (Strange were the medical practices of the ancients.) No one in the Court of Wu was willing to do that, not even the Prince. Only the King of Yue volunteered. The King of Wu recovered after this somewhat unconventional treatment. He was so moved by this demonstration of unswerving loyalty on the part of Yue's king that he released him to return to his own country.

Yue's king had endured shame and disgrace normally beyond the limits of human capacity. Upon his return, he set to work on a twenty-year plan for revenge. He encouraged his countrymen and women to give birth over the first ten years to increase the population, and for the next ten years to raise and train the youngsters. Upon the advice of his Prime Minister, he also gave gifts to Wu throughout these years to express his devotion. The King of Yue paid high prices to purchase grain from Wu, leaving Wu without any grain in reserve, and he sent beautiful women to serve in the court of Wu. King Wu was content in the soft arms of Xi Si (a present from Yue and one of the four most beautiful women in the history of China) and he ignored state affairs. Yue also sent the best craftsmen and architects to Wu, so the King of Wu started to spend large sums of money on construction and exhausted his state treasury. Yue used spies to divide the Court staff and trick them into betraying and killing each other.

During these twenty years, the King of Yue slept on a pile of wood chips and would daily lick a pig's bile to remind him of the bitterness of defeat and of his revenge. Finally, when the time was right, he attacked Wu. Wu's King begged for his life and declared his willingness to become a servant of the King of Yue, but Yue forced Wu's King to kill himself.

Another example involves Sun Bin, the brilliant military strategist who played the three horses game. He understood the value of pretending to be lowly, naive, and stupid. After his classmate chopped off Sun Bin's feet and imprisoned him in the country of Wei because he feared future competition from him, Sun Bin pretended to be a crazy idiot to lessen the fear and lower the guard of his classmate. When Chi's ambassador visited Wei, Sun Bin used him to make a clever escape, and later destroyed Wei and put his classmate, the commander of the Wei army, to death.

Conclusion: In all of Asian culture, this strategy is especially popular. The testing of a hero is not when he is eating the tiger, but it is rather the period of endurance, his acceptance of disgrace by acting like a pig. To endure beyond any normal human's capacity is the true proof of real manhood.

Sun Tzu's Art of War (Chapter 1) says, when the enemy is strong, one must be careful in making preparations. One should avoid strength and attack weakness. When one is capable, he must feign being incapable.

Strategy 28 - Cross the River and Destroy the Bridge

A bridge is useful for crossing a river. Once the river is crossed, if there is no need for return, the bridge can become a liability. In Chinese history, the people who suffered hardships and sacrificed greatly for new rulers, those who supported and contributed the most to a new regime, often ended up dead. These supporters were like the bridge, no longer useful and ready to be destroyed. The claim of expected rewards for loyalty brought inevitable destruction.

Two loyal and able aides, without whom the King of Yue could not have conquered the country of Wu, became liabilities. One was given a short time in which to leave the country and the second aide was eventually killed.

To further illustrate: after Liu Bang united China, establishing the Han Dynasty, one of his three valuable assistants chose to leave. One of the remaining men was jailed and the third man was chopped into meat sauce. All were effectively removed from the possibility of becoming competition.

Conclusion: The leader needs strong supporters when he is fighting to achieve a goal. Once the goal is achieved, these same adherents, because of their superior abilities and talents, may be considered liabilities. Smart Chinese learn the importance of timing, and leave before the party is over.

Strategy 31 - The Beauty Trap

The practice of using the opposite sex as a means of accomplishing objectives has been used concurrently with spy operations, military intrigue, and bribery. The story of the King of Yue's revenge contains the earliest recorded instance of the use of beauty for purposes of spying. As you have read, the King of Yue sent Xi Si, one of the four most beautiful women in the history of China, to Wu's king. Xi Si was the childhood lover of Yue's Prime Minister. She felt that duty to her country and the opportunity to gain power and revenge for her King was greater than any of her personal preferences.

In the old Chinese social structure, family honor and regard for one's country have the highest priority among the life's duties. Xi Si captured the King of Wu's affections to the extent that he let down his guard. Yue thus established an effective spy network which led to the eventual destruction of Wu.

Even in today's business world, the gift of "women" is not uncommon in Asian societies. It is the host's or seller's duty to tacitly understand the desires of the guest or buyer. There are specially trained women to serve men's pleasures. The Asian businessman feels comfortable in this atmosphere. The barrier between host and guest, buyer and seller, may thus be removed and a close business relationship achieved.

Conclusion: In every part of history, in the East and West, there are instances of sex being used as an effective tool when employed with care. It requires planning and guidance. When used wrongly, there is a Chinese proverb which says, "You can lose your maiden as well as your troops." In general, Asian society feels that female power can be very effective. Thus, the saying: "Woman is water, and man is mud. They mix well together."

Strategy 32 - Empty City

During the Three Kingdom period (220-265 A.D.), Zhu Ge Liang sent his troops out to battle. His city was left without good protection. His greatest enemy, Si Ma, the commander of the army of Wei, made an unexpected approach while Zhu Ge Liang was in this weak position. Zhu Ge Liang used the "empty city" for his protection. An old man was sent to open the city's front gate and sweep the entrance way. Zhu Ge Liang then went to the tower to prepare food and wine. He played a musical instrument and sang poetry as if he had not a care in the world.

Commander Si Ma approached the city gates, but hesitated to enter. He was wary of tricks and feared a trap was waiting because of this obvious display of lowered security. Si Ma ordered his troops to retreat and wait so he might discover the true situation. Meanwhile, Zhu Ge Liang's soldiers returned from their battles and the city was once more defended.

The Spring and Autumn Annals cite similar incidents occurring seven hundred years earlier and five hundred years later than the Zhu Ge Liang story. Unlike Zhu Ge Liang's "empty city," the beleaguered cities were not always free of traps and ambush. During the Tang Dynasty (618-907 A.D.), Northern barbarians attacked the city of Gua in Gansu Province and killed the commander. The Emperor sent a new commander named Zhang. Zhang arrived and attempted to rebuild the damaged city walls. The barbarians prepared to attack again before the fortifications were put in order. Zhang was able to use the "empty city" strategy with great success. He opened all the city's gates. Like Si Ma, fearing a trap, the barbarians returned home.

Conclusion: A deliberate display of weakness can conceal one's true strength and confuse the enemy. Creating a mystery by hiding your real strength is a viable strategic weapon.

Strategy 35 - Chain Link or Combination

Chain link strategies are the combining of all tricks, devices and schemes into one interconnected arrangement, like the links of a chain. Each link or plan can be individual or tied into connecting links (or plans) until the enemy is totally demoralized and defeated.

Dong Zou held the power in China during the Han Dynasty. He was an excessively cruel person. After inviting members of the Court to a party, he would display captured enemy soldiers, behead them, chop off their hands or feet, or poke out their eyes. Bloodshed did not move him. He would go about the party as if nothing out of the ordinary were happening. Court members felt that sooner or later they would all become victims of Dong Zou. He was too strong to plot against. He had total control over the Emperor, and the protection of his brave and loyal stepson, Lu Bu, one of China's military heroes. There seemed no way to remove the tyrant.

Wong Yuen, a man with no soldiers or weapons, was determined to find a way to overthrow Dong Zou. He knew both Dong Zou and Lu Bu had a weakness for beautiful women, and Wong Yuen designed a strategy to use this weakness. Diao Chan was Wong Yuen's very beautiful stepdaughter. Wong Yuen invited Lu Bu to his house and had his stepdaughter serve tea. Yuen then gave Lu Bu and Diao Chan time alone. Lu Bu was very taken by Diao Chan's beauty and asked for her hand in marriage. Wong Yuen agreed. Wong Yuen then invited Dong Zou to his home. When Dong Zou met Yuen's beautiful stepdaughter, he was also attracted to her and wanted to take Diao Chan as one of his wives. Wong Yuen also agreed to this. Both men thought they were the only one who had the hand of Diao Chan.

Dong Zou immediately married Diao Chan. Lu Bu could not protest marriage. Dong Zou was his stepfather and Chinese ways required that Lu Bu respect the elder's wishes. Dong Zou was very happy in the tender arms of Diao Chan. But Diao Chan was secretly seeing Lu Bu. She told Lu Bu that she was living in hell every day with Dong Zou, that she could not be happy with this "old man." She chastised Lu Bu by telling him that, although he was a great hero of China, he couldn't even save her from this misery and suffering. Lu Bu arranged a trap for his stepfather and killed Dong Zou, thus ending the tyrant's grip on China.

This event used the Beauty Trap, and the Fire Burning Across the River. A conflict of interest arose between the two men when they fell in love with one beautiful woman. The conflict was a fire burning between Dong Zou and Lu Bu. Then, Wong Yuen borrowed Lu Bu's Hand to Kill his stepfather. Wong Yuen used a set of strategies (chain link) to accomplish his goal.

Conclusion: Each of the strategies separately or all 36 together can be used to create confusion in the mind of your enemy.

Strategy 36 - Escape is the Best Policy

When faced with unfavorable conditions, retreat. Attack when conditions are more favorable. In order to attain the ultimate victory, it is sometimes necessary to accept a temporary defeat, and by escaping, preserve one's fighting strength. For some though, it may be more difficult to accept the shame of retreat than to die with glory.

Chinese history holds many examples of escape. The founders of many of the Chinese Dynasties were masters of escape. The founder of the Han Dynasty, Liu Bang, escaped repeatedly throughout his life as a commander. Before Liu Bang united China by defeating Xiang Yu, he spent four unsuccessful years warring against Xiang Yu. Each time Liu Bang was defeated, he retreated and awaited a more favorable time to attack anew. Xiang Yu, on the other hand, was only defeated by Liu Bang once. Once was enough for one who did not understand the art of escape. To save face, Xiang Yu took his own life on the banks of the Wu River.

In ancient China, in such a large land mass, if one could not win a battle immediately, escape was usually easy. China has many places in which to hide. One simply had to retreat to where one could not be found. Escape became a wise thing to do. The Chinese have learned the art of thick face. They can accept disgrace when envisioning a long-range victory. Chinese battles tended to drag on for years, with each defeat followed by a successful retreat. The battle between Liu Bang and Xiang Yu lasted for five years, from 206 to 202 B.C. Escaping may not be heroic, but it does insure that one can fight another day.

Chinese aphorisms: "A good man does not fight a losing battle." "Keep a green mountain and you will not fear the lack of firewood." The second statement means as long as you keep yourself from danger by maintaining your necessary supplies (firewood), you still have a chance for victory.

In Japan, there is no room to escape and regroup. Once something is started, it must be finished because there is no place to go. Therefore the Japanese developed quite different battle strategies. When faced with the possibility of defeat, the Chinese would use ingenious means to live to fight another day while the Japanese developed a philosophy of death before dishonor. While the Japanese and Chinese share many other psychological values, they differ on this point.

Conclusion

This last strategy of the 36 is the most popular. All Chinese school children know this one. The Chinese feel, "If I can fight and win, I will fight. If I cannot win, I will escape." This strategy has been mastered by the Chinese, but not the Japanese. In business practice, this strategy is often expressed as: "Retreat is another form of advance." Remember that Chinese are always on the advance regardless of how their actions appear.

These strategies have been illustrated by classical examples drawn from Chinese history. However, in most day-to-day situations, they will not be so clearly delineated. Each theme may manifest through an infinite set of variations. Only upon careful examination will one be able to pierce the outward, camouflaging forms to detect the essence of the actual strategy being used.

9 THE WISDOM OF THE CHINESE

At one time or another, most Westerners have heard that the Chinese people have a tradition of being very wise. The Chinese people accept this as true without embarrassment or false modesty. They believe themselves to be a sage and intelligent people, and feel that their wisdom and intelligence have influenced China's neighboring countries.

The Chinese believe the purpose of learning the 36 strategies is to be able to identify when the deceptions are being used on you. The purpose of learning the Art of War is to create the highest form of victory: to conquer without resorting to physical violence.

The following stories show how the Chinese freely use their inner wisdom in almost every aspect of daily life.

The Chinese Art of Persuasion

The King of Chu in the Warring State period had a beautiful horse which he loved greatly. The King made clothes for the horse and built a beautiful house for the animal to live in. The horse even had a beautiful carved bed to sleep in. The king, of course, fed the horse the finest food available. This made the horse fat and it died. The King wanted to buy a coffin to bury his beloved horse and he wanted to use a burial ceremony traditionally reserved for government officials. The people felt this was all too much for a horse and so his advisers told the King. The King announced that anyone suggesting he not to do these things for his horse would be killed.

News of the King's announcement traveled to a man called You Mon. You Mon went to Court to see the King of Chu. You Mon cried profusely as he walked in and the King asked him what was wrong. You Mon said that this horse, which the king proposed to bury as a government official, was the most beloved thing of his King and country. You Mon told the King he thought such a burial was not good enough for the horse and he thought the horse should be buried as a lord. You Mon said the horse should have a carved jade casket. The casket should be carried in intricately carved wood and the wood should be the special wood of the Emperor. Soldiers should dress for the funeral and notices should be dispatched to neighboring countries for them to send representatives. You Mon told the King they should have cows, sheep, and pigs in the temples to worship. This would let the kings and lords of other lands know he thought little of mankind, but gave great respect to horses.

As King Chu listened to You Won, he realized his folly. He asked You Won what he could do to make things right. You Won told the King to bury his horse according to the way livestock should be buried -- in the human stomach. The King of Chu took You Won's advice, cooked the horse, and shared it with all his people.

During the Warring State period, the country of Jien was thinking of attacking the neighboring country of Wei. A lord of Jien laughed in court. The King of Jien asked the lord what he found so funny. The lord explained to the king, "I saw a neighbor of mine the other day who sent his wife to somebody else's household. On his way to deliver his wife, the man saw a very attractive woman on the road. The man stopped to talk with the attractive woman and flirted with her. As he was busy flirting, he turned his head and noticed his wife speaking sweetly with a man who was also passing on the street. She was flirting with him. I cannot help secretly laughing at the situation."

The King of Jien realized the story was meant for him. If the King takes his troops to attack Wei, there are other countries ready to move their troops into Jien while he is absent. The King of Jien gave up the attack on Wei. It takes a very clever man to present his ideas and persuade a king. It also takes a very wise man to hear a story, understand the hidden message, and take proper action because of it.

During the Warring State period, Chin attacked the country of Zao. Zao sent for help from the country of Chi. Chi insisted as a condition of sending troops to help Zao, that it be given the prince of Zao, Chang An Jun, as hostage. Prince Chang An Jun was the youngest and most beloved son of the Empress Queen Mother, who was a powerful lady in Court. Although court advisers tried to persuade her to send Chang An Jun to Chi, she held firm and would not allow it. The Empress Queen Mother eventually let it be known that, if anybody mentioned sending her young son to Chi again, she would spit in their face. Nobody dared broach the subject with the Empress Queen Mother again.

An old court advisor by the name of Chu was willing to see the Empress one more time about her son going to Chi. The Empress greeted him with great anger on her face. Chu walked slowly towards the Empress Queen Mother and sat down. He walked slowly to show her that he had nothing important on his mind, that he was not in a hurry. Chu told the Empress Queen Mother that he had been ill.

Chu said, "I am sick and my feet do not feel good. I also am worried about my Empress. How are you feeling? Are receiving proper care?" Chu was very casual. He had just come for a regular visit.

The Empress Queen Mother told Chu that she was not feeling very well. She too was having trouble with her feet.

Chu asked how her appetite was and the Empress Queen Mother told him that she was able to eat only a little rice cereal. Chu told her that he was not eating very well either. Chu said, "I eat enough to keep myself alive and I walk a little bit every day." The Empress Queen Mother told Chu, "I cannot even walk."

They were getting along quite well. The defensive attitude of the Empress Queen Mother was lessening. Chu said, "I have a young child, a son. He is not very able. I am getting old and I need to make plans for him. Can you take him as a guard to serve you?" The Empress readily agreed and she asked Chu how old the boy was. "He is fifteen. I would like him to stay with me for a while because he is so young, but before I die, I would very much like to see him in a secure position."

The Empress was surprised at Chu's attitude towards his son. She said, "You men also love your sons?" "Of course we do," said Chu. "We love them even more than their mothers." The Empress laughed at this and said, "This is strange. Why do you think fathers love their sons more than mothers?" Chu answered, "Because, just between you and me, I think you love the princess, Ian, more than you love Prince Chang An Jun. The Empress Queen Mother said, "That is not true. My favorite son is the young prince, Chang An Jun." Chu explained, "Parents love their children and make long-term plans for them. Remember when you said goodbye to Princess Ian and sent her to be wed in the country of Ian. You cried. After she married the King of Ian, you hoped and prayed that she would not offend the king and be sent back home and that nothing bad would happen to her. You had great plans that Princess Ian's children and the generations to come would be the heirs of the country of Ian."

The Empress agreed. Chu continued, "When we look back at the generations in the country of Zao and other neighboring countries, the lords and kings have bestowed wealth and high positions on their children. Yet, few have kept them. This is because these heirs were granted wealth and position without having to earn it. They never had to establish themselves or labor for their countries. They had everything they wanted just given to them. Today you have given Prince Chang An Jun beautiful land, respectable titles and wealth. Now there is an opportunity for Prince Chang An Jun to serve his country by going to Chi, but you will not let him go. What will happen when you die? Who is going to provide for Prince Chang An Jun? You are not thinking in the long term for Prince Chang An Jun as you have for Princess Ian.

The Empress Queen Mother understood what Chu was saying and she asked Chu to make arrangements for her son to go to Chi. Chang An Jun went to the country of Chi as hostage and Chi in turn helped Zao, and the country of Zao was saved from the attack by Chin.

The King of Chu asked Mr. Song, "Is there a problem with your character? Why do so many people speak ill of you?" Mr. Song answered, "Yes, my Lord. I hope my gracious Lord will forgive me and let me explain. In the old time, a man came to a city and sang a popular song. The tune was easy to carry, and thousands of people in the city followed his lead and sang the tune with him. Later, the man introduced a new song. It had a more complicated melody, and only a few hundred people were able to harmonize and sing along with him. Later still, he introduced another melody which was even more difficult. Only a few dozen people were able to sing with him. Finally, he composed a song so complicated that only a handful of people could understand the music and sing with him. So, my Lord, how can the average person know what my character is."

Tien Wen served under the King of Wei as premier. General Wu of Wei was a great Chinese military strategist. General Wu felt his contributions to the country should make his station in life higher than that of Tien Wen. General Wu broached the subject with Premier Tien Wen.

General Wu said, "Let's compare, between you and me, who has made the greatest contribution to our country. I command the military forces and am able to motivate soldiers to die for our country. I am able to control our country's enemies and prevent them from invading. You or me; who has contributed more?" Premier Tien Wen said, "In this, of course you are better."

General Wu continued, "I guard the west river against the strong army of Chin and I am also able to have our neighboring country defer to us as their superiors. In this, who is better?" Premier Tien Wen answered, "In this, you are."

"I manage the staffs and officials and am very popular with the people. They support me and this results in our country being orderly and wealthy. In this, who is better?" General Wu asked. "In this also, you are better," answered Premier Tien Wen.

General Wu looked puzzled. "In all these things, you say I am better than you. Yet your position is higher than mine. Why is this so?"

Premier Tien Wen explained, "When our Lord of Wei was young, no one in court backed him. They were suspicious and did not trust him. Even the common people failed to support him. But I served him loyally and helped him establish the country of Wei into the nation we know today. Without my work, you would not have been able to build your glories, as the country would not have been. That is why my position is higher than yours."

General Wu fell silent, finally understanding the disparity between his position and that of Premier Tien Wen. The contributions Premier Tien Wen had made to the country of Wei were indeed great.

Exchange Small For Large

In the Warring State period, the King of Chin lost a precious horse. It was later discovered that the horse had been found by village people who cooked and ate it. When the news reached the King's soldiers, they captured the village people. The King of Chin said, "A good lord does not punish his people for something they have done to an animal. From what I understand, after you eat good horse meat, you must drink some wine. It is bad for your health not to." So King of Chin did not hand out punishment; instead, he passed out wine for the villagers to drink and let them go free.

A year later, the country of Chin was short of food and Chin's representatives went to the country of Jien to ask for grain. Jien saw Chin's famine condition as an opportunity to attack, and they engaged in battle. The King of Chin was surrounded by Jien's troops. He was injured and had no way of escaping. Suddenly, volunteer troops charged into the enemy camp of Jien, freed the King of Chin, and captured the King of Jien. These volunteer troops were the village people who had eaten the king's horse a year before.

Farsighted

When Prime Minister Yei of the Tang Dynasty lay dying, he counseled his children. "Prime Minister Zhang and I have never gotten along. After I die, he will come to my funeral. You must display all of my jade pieces. He loves jade ornaments. Now, if he does not look at them, it will mean he harbors a very deep hatred for me and will try to hurt you children. If he shows interest and looks at my jade ornaments, then you should ask him if he would be so kind as to write a few words for my tombstone. Zhang's love of jade will bring the best out in him and he will write good things. You should immediately prepare a tombstone. As soon as he finishes writing the words, have them engraved onto the stone and show the stone to the

Emperor. Prime Minister Zhang often sees things differently after he thinks about them for a while. A few days after he has written the words, he is going to feel sorry that he wrote good things about me and ask for his writing back. Then, you will tell him that it has already been engraved and approved by the Emperor."

A few days later, Prime Minister Yei died and Zhang showed up at the funeral just as predicted. He enjoyed examining the late Prime Minister's jade ornaments, so Yei's children asked him to write a few words for their father's gravestone. Zhang sat down, picked up a brush, and wrote kind words about Prime Minister Yei. A few days later, Zhang sent a messenger to Yei's children. Zhang said he felt the words he wrote were inappropriate and would like to change them. Yei's children showed the messenger the engraved stone and explained that the Emperor had already approved it.

Zhang wrote kind words about Prime Minister Yei at the funeral because he was moved by the surroundings and his love for jade. When he learned his words had already been reviewed by the Emperor, Zhang realized he could not change his statement and speak ill of Yei's past activities to the Emperor in order to put harm on Yei's children (in old time China, the punishment of high treason was not limited only to the person who committed the crime, but to all of his blood relatives) so the children were saved. Zhang later discovered he had been tricked by Prime Minister Yei, but he could do nothing about it. The Chinese often are very deep thinkers. They even consider what will transpire after they die and prepare for the consequences.

The Emperor of Tang spoke to one of his advisors. The Emperor said, " I know General Lee knows how to use soldiers, but do you think we will be able to control General Lee in the long run? I am the only one who has control over him now. I am worried that when the young prince succeeds me as Emperor; he will not be able to control him at all."

The Emperor's advisor said, "I think the best thing to do is discharge General Lee from Court. When the young prince becomes Emperor, he can restore General Lee again to favor. Out of gratitude, the general will serve him loyally." The Emperor found a small excuse and discharged General Lee and sent him home. When his son became Emperor, he recalled Lee as the head military commander, under which title he served the new Emperor loyally.

During the Han Dynasty, the Emperor of Han had a favorite lady called Madam Lee. The Emperor came to visit Madam Lee who was gravely ill. She covered her head and said, "I am sick and due to my sickness, my face has become unpleasant. I do not wish you to see me. I would like to ask a favor of you, however, that you take care of my two brothers for me."

The Emperor said, "Madam, I know you are very ill, and you might not be able to get up again. Please let me see you one more time, and then we will talk about your brothers." Madam Lee again refused.

The Emperor said, "Let me see you one time. I will give you gold, and I will grant high positions to your brothers." Madam Lee said, "Whether you grant my brothers positions or not is up to you, but I cannot see you." The Emperor was not pleased and walked away with great sadness.

Madam Lee's sisters were very unhappy. They asked her why she had not allowed the Emperor to see her and thereby accept his offer of high positions for her brothers. Madam Lee explained, "I could not let the Emperor see me because I do wish for my brothers to have high positions. I served the Emperor with my beauty and my charm. Now my beauty and charm have faded, so the love the Emperor has for me will lessen if he sees me. Then, why would he help my brothers."

After Madam Lee's death, the Emperor could not forget her. He used the ceremony of the queens to bury her. He wrote poetry in her memory and granted high positions to her brothers.

In the Tang Dynasty, a man named Kuo held a high position in Court. When Kuo received guests, he invariably gathered his household ladies into the living room. One day, when a man came to see him, Kuo asked everyone to leave the house. They didn't understand why

Kuo was asking them to leave, and they asked him about it. Kuo told them, "This visitor has a very ugly face. If my household ladies see him, they will giggle. If then he comes into power in the future, there will be no place for me because his face and heart are equally ugly." This is an example of the Chinese seeing to the smallest detail to prevent future harm from coming to them.

There is another story of the wisdom of Kuo. Kuo's house was always open. People could come and go as they pleased. Kuo was not in the habit of asking who was in his household. Kuo's brother asked him why he was so open. Kuo explained, "I have 300 people caring for my horses. Another 1,000 support my household at government expense. If these people are suppressed, if they are intimidated by walls they cannot enter, they may feel displeasure in their hearts. If they become jealous and want to harm me, they will be able to destroy me and there will be nothing I can do about it. I let them do what they want. They can enter, they can leave. My house has no secrets. So, even if a devious person wanted to damage my reputation and reported false statements to the Emperor, the Emperor and other high level officials would not believe the accusations because my family is like an open book."

Judgment

The King of Chi had ten ladies he favored after his wife died. Nobody knew who was the King's favorite among the ten. This was known only by the King himself. A man named Shiue thought to himself, "If I can discover which of the ten ladies is my Lord's favorite, then I can advise him to marry that one. The King will then trust my judgment and he will listen to my advice in the future. I will become the King's confidant."

Shiue devised a plan. He made ten pairs of jade earrings, one of them particularly beautiful. He gave all ten to the King and asked the King to give them to the ladies. The next day, Shiue watched to see which lady had received the most beautiful pair, and he advised the King to make her his queen.

The King of Chu, during the Warring State period established San as prince. Later, rumors circulated that he wished to establish Zhi as his prince and eliminate San. Prince San asked his teacher how he could discover whether the rumors were true. San's teacher advised him to invite the King's confidant to dinner and deliberately be rude to him. Prince San followed his teacher's advice. The King's confidant accepted Prince San's invitation for dinner, and San was exceedingly rude to him. The King's confidant reacted with great anger and told San, "No wonder the King wants to kill you and establish Zhi as prince."

If San was still desired as a prince by the King, his abuse and ill manners would have been tolerated by others close to the King. If he was no longer desired as a prince, they would not tolerate his impolite behavior. So, San reported back to his teacher of the confidant's great anger, and the teacher arranged to have the King killed.

King Solomon's Match

Here are several stories about fighting for the ownership of sons. They show wisdom which compares with King Solomon.

In a story from the Han Dynasty, two brothers lived in the same house. Both their wives were pregnant. The elder brother's wife lost her baby while the younger brother's wife gave birth to a son. The elder brother's wife stole the younger brother's baby. They eventually went to court to resolve the conflict. They argued their cases for three years but no decision was made as to whose child the boy was. A new judge came in who ordered soldiers to bring the baby to court. The judge asked the two ladies to walk ten steps from the child and then instructed them both to rush towards the boy and grab him. The elder brother's wife got hold of the child and wouldn't let go. She fought with great force. The boy cried, so the younger brother's wife became afraid that her son was being hurt so she let go. The new judge, observing the ladies, instantly decided the child belonged to the younger brother.

Two men were fighting over a length of silk. They each claimed it as their own. The judge ordered the silk cut, gave each man half, and sent them home. Then the judge had two people secretly follow each man and watch. One man was delighted. He had gained something. The other man was very upset. He had lost something that had belonged to him. The judge had the happy man arrested and sent to jail.

Just outside of town, a man was robbed of three bundles of silk he was taking to market. He returned and reported the robbery to the judge. He described the robber's clothes and the horse the robber was riding. The judge sent a notice that a person dressed in the clothes and riding a horse matching the description given of the robber had been killed. The notice said the man could not be identified and asked his family to come claim the body. An old woman answered the notice. She cried and said her son fit the description of the man killed. The judge then sent people to capture the woman's son and recover the lost silk.

Through these stories, we are given a rare glimpse of how a rich and convoluted, historically-oriented civilization such as China has given life to the messages passed from one generation to the next, creating an accumulated body of human understanding and wisdom to draw upon for daily guidance and inspiration.

10 POSITION FOR SUCCESS

It may seem nearly impossible for a Westerner to develop a strategy that will take advantage of the aforementioned Chinese peculiarities and traits, but this is not necessarily the case. If the Westerner is willing to apply heart and head to the task by altering his normal conceptual framework to permit an alternative view of reality, he can learn to use the techniques of the Chinese as a Chinese would use them. By learning to like the Chinese, by gaining awareness of the Chinese mind and attitudes on life, the understanding will come. The following sections present a few more examples of Chinese business practices which may provide additional help in assimilating the Chinese view of the marketplace.

Control, Control, Control

In the Sechuan province, in the city of Chongqing, there is a tourist hotel which was built under a joint venture between a group of Chinese and a group of American businessmen. The hotel's general manager was a well qualified American hotel expert who was employed at the request of the Americans as a device to protect the interests of the foreign investors. This seemed a sensible move. However, a year later, the hotel board, which was made up entirely of Chinese members, fired the general manager. They informed their U.S. partners that it was necessary to fire the American general manager because he did not speak Chinese and had no understanding of the Chinese culture and ways.

What exactly did the Chinese mean with this accusation? The American did not speak Chinese when he was employed. Are we to assume the Chinese were ignorant of this fact? They approved his employment at the time of hiring. And they approved it apparently because of his expertise in hotel management, not because he was an expert in Chinese culture. Obviously, the real reasons the Chinese fired this individual were not presented.

The real mistake made by the American general manager and his superiors was in believing the publicity put forth by the Chinese about the "New China's" attitude towards economic reform. Despite all the good intentions in the higher levels of Chinese government, when it comes to day-to-day reforms in business, we find an entirely different story.

Chinese management groups work under the principle of "Guan Guan Sian Hu," which means that officials protect each others' interests. This concept has existed for thousands of years. The concept of economic reform is barely ten years old.

When the reform is translated into daily life it means the loss of special privileges, working harder and longer hours, and having to take on more responsibility for the same compensation. This was not what Chinese management had in mind when they first heard about economic reform.

The abovementioned Chinese who went into the joint venture with the Americans had already received their "prize." They had convinced the foreigners to give them funds to build the hotel, they were able to take control of its management, and they foresaw outright ownership in the near future. They could now comfortably pat themselves on the shoulder for a job well done. They reasoned that if the hotel lost money because of firing the American hotel expert, that would just encourage the foreigners to give up their interests earlier and thus would return the hotel to their ownership sooner.

In order to finalize the original agreement with the Americans, the Chinese felt they had to agree to the Westerners' request to place their expert in the general manager position. But the Chinese also suspected the foreign expert would become a real problem in their lives by taking his job too seriously and would create unnecessary demands regarding standards of performance. They also suspected he would attempt the removal of all their customary privileges.

It is common for Chinese businessmen to believe a statement I have heard many times: "We never take any harsh or hasty actions against nonproductive individuals, since one never knows what high official may be related to that individual."

The American expert's integrity caused him to step on some toes which caused displeasure among the Chinese board members. Nevertheless, the biggest problem these foreign investors ran into was their lack of control over the whole project. They should never have agreed to the entirely Chinese board. This was the root cause of all of their later problems. In order for a joint venture between Chinese and Westerners to have any chance of success in China, absolute operational control by the Westerners is a must. It is necessary to control the controllers, particularly at the board level.

Even setting up the relationship on a 50-50 basis is ineffective because the host country always has the advantage of time and territory. Often a work stoppage or confrontation will result in financial loss due to an inability on the part of the Westerner to made appropriate and timely changes.

According to an insider who wishes to remain anonymous, there were two main reasons for the firing of the American expert. If he had been able to learn more about Chinese culture before taking up his responsibilities as general manager, he would have saved himself and his company a great deal of trouble.

The first involved the fact that Chinese high officials have a habit of drinking and eating at company expense. This was not tolerated by the American expert. To drink and eat at company expense has been the way in China for a long, long time; almost from the beginning of Chinese history. It is considered to be one of the privileges which come with a job. It is done for two basic reasons. The most obvious is the need to promote public relations or business by entertaining. But, the deeper unspoken reason is the income level of the officials. In general the lifestyle of these officials is very humble at home. (Of course this indicates their virtue as it shows they do not take unauthorized income from other sources.) So, entertaining at government or company expense is a method of self-fulfillment.

A commonly used phrase in China is "Ta Yia Gi" which means to eat to your hearts content. "Ta Yia Gi" at government or company expense is expected and is merely one of the special privileges which come with a job in this socialist society. It is difficult to remove a practice which has been in place for so many years. Even the Chinese government has attempted to discourage this practice since the bills they pay because of "Ta Yia Gi" are enormous. They have also tried to discourage travel at government expense, but to no avail. As always, change comes slow to China.

One time I was scheduled to visit seven provinces and ten cities, all at government expense. I requested that I not be entertained lavishly. I find this very time-consuming and wasteful. The central government official to whom I spoke appreciated and thanked me for my sense of moderation. He said, "Yes, we are a poor country so please tell those who accompany you to inform the local officials to not be wasteful." Of course, they all ignored this message since time-honored practice means much more than mere words. Each meal still took three hours.

These people were aware that my American guest and I preferred to not eat certain foods such as turtle soup, roast turtle, and crickets, but persisted in serving these foods anyway. In fact, one host served turtle soup for five meals over a three- day period. A Chinese businessman spoke with me once about the prevalence of waste among Chinese officials when entertaining. He said they will order the most exotic and expensive foods (the price of turtle is approximately $30 per pound), knowing that in most cases the foreign guest will not touch them. He believes they use the foreign guests merely as an excuse to fulfill their own desires.

Along with his disapproval of eating on the company bill, the American hotel expert also fired over one hundred workers who did not meet his standards. Among those fired were children of some high officials, a very bad move in China.

It is important to always remember that the plan of the Chinese is to pressure you into giving them money. It is up to you to ensure a return on your investment. The time to gain control is, therefore, before you give them any money. Always have over 50% control of the board and 100% control of the operational procedures. Build in incentive programs for the workers and control the hiring and firing of personnel.

These are some of the new suggestions that the Chinese government has designed to encourage foreign companies to gain greater control of their projects. However, these do not come automatically by doing business in China but rather are gained through skillful negotiation with the Chinese.

Trust

Business is never just business in any Asian country. In China, this is true more than anywhere else. In Chapter One you learned something about the meaning of friendship in China. But a friend in China is also someone with whom one can work out a problem. The time and effort one invests to establish that trust and friendship will be handsomely rewarded. Among all the Chinese people I have encountered all over the world, those in China have been the most eager to be friends with their foreign guests

Yet an American executive expressed to me that he has not found the Chinese to offer genuine friendship, except in one instance. It is my contention that such actions are due to their ulterior motive of usually developing such a relationship to aquire status. But, if you offer genuine friendship to the Chinese at a sustained level, you will find it returned many-fold when they learn to trust you.

The Spouse

As you learned in Chapter 4, the men of China are generally wife-fearing and are definitely not ashamed of it. When doing business in China, unless you have a very close personal relationship, you seldom have the opportunity of meeting a Chinese associate's wife. In a socialist state such as mainland China, the wife usually has her own professional interests, hence the tradition of bringing the wife along as a social ornament in business gatherings has not developed here.

However, in Hong Kong, Taiwan, and Singapore, you will have more opportunity to meet spouses at a social gathering. Always pay special attention to the wives. I have found that wives may not help your business position but can certainly damage it if you get on the wrong side of them.

The Chinese woman wields a great deal of power and importance within her home as well as without. But beware! Do not try to make points with her by giving her a compliment about her beauty or femininity. Such a gesture is considered to be taking advantage of her by your words. It is known to the Chinese as "Chi Tofu" which means "Eat tofu." (Yes, that's tofu as in bean curd.) No one seems to know where the saying came from, but it is such an offensive act it can be considered to be a form of mental rape. Even though all women love to be complimented, unless the lady is under ten years old, you enter a danger zone if you attempt to compliment her without having certain knowledge of her temperament.

Smart Bargaining

Chinese are very price-sensitive when it comes to purchasing goods from abroad. The old concept of "compare prices with no less than three suppliers" is the standard practice of the Chinese government. As a matter of fact, on just about any sizeable purchase, the Chinese have already shopped all over the world. They will use the information gained to play one company against the others. They already have proposals from all of your competitors and understand very well how low they can get you to go.

There is another factor which is even more important than the price and that is the question of terms. Chinese, when making the purchase, like to have the feeling they are not really paying for the goods. Terms such as barter or buy now, pay later (the later the better) or very long payment terms and very low interest are the most attractive.

Hang In

Doing business in China is a slow, grinding process. But there is good news. If you are the partner the Chinese have chosen to "grind" it out with, then stay with it -- hang in there. The chances are great that your persistence will be rewarded financially.

A Chinese official told me, "We may spend more time in concluding a business arrangement than other international companies, but we have often decided with whom we wish to do business before the agreement is reached. That is why we spend a large amount of time working out our differences. Conversely, the Western company is usually looking for the company with whom they can agree. That is the difference in our business style."

Heed my warning! Avoid any type of showdown. The key to concluding your business deal in China is persistence -- hang in there. Just like going to battle, one must prepare to fight a long war. If there are enough favourable elements existing which indicate victory is possible, one must know how to conserve resources and utilize them efficiently and effectively.

Eliminate Misunderstandings

It takes relentless determination to weed out all possible cultural, language, business style, and conceptual barriers which may lead to unnecessary difficulties in your business dealings.

Clarify any important agreement. Make sure both parties are holding the same mental pictures. This may sound juvenile, but it pays to be juvenile in this case, if that is what it is.

A Western auto maker went into a joint venture with a group in China. Due to lack of foreign currency, the Chinese suggested barter of goods as a portion of the payment. The negotiator for the Western company thought, "Why not? We can always use leather for auto interiors, and China is a very large exporter of leather."

However, the Chinese forgot to mention that barter to them does not mean anything China can produce, but is limited to those items available to the auto maker. And leather was not one of them. If an item is of high demand for international trading, it will be in short supply to the domestic market. The people who produce the leather export their goods for hard foreign currency and are not about to sell it to a domestic auto maker who will pay only Chinese currency. The Chinese auto maker told me that they have difficulty getting Westerners to understand this simple problem.

Be Flexible and Creative

A Western company working in China must be flexible and creative. In another words, you must think on your feet. Make sure your terms are realistic and workable in the environment of China. This does not mean one must sacrifice the integrity of the project, or that the Western company should give in to the demands of the Chinese. But do consider the people with whom you are dealing and realize there are certain terms which will never work in China.

In the West, there is more than one way to skin a cat. In China, there is more than one way to tame a dragon. Often the Chinese are very receptive to creative suggestions. They know they are not as knowledgeable in the world of high finance as Westerners. If you make sensible suggestions, accompanied by careful explanations, you will be surprised at the wonderful results you can achieve.

Status

When you look at a Chinese business card, you will often find many titles besides the title which indicates what the bearer does for living. The president of a large Asian food company has four titles on the front of his business card along with his and his company's name. On the back, he has over twenty more titles listed. It is customary in Asian society to flaunt your prestigious associations. This includes Japan, Korea, The Philippines and, of course, China, Taiwan, Hong Kong and Singapore.

Effective Unofficial Communication Pipeline

It is not an easy task for the Westerner to understand the Chinese, nor is it easy for the Chinese to understand the Westerner. There are natural linguistic, social, and cultural barriers. The Chinese are naturally more comfortable with other Chinese because they share the same culture. Chinese believe China is not merely a place on Earth, it is a place in the heart. The Chinese prefer to work through individuals -- persons they can talk to and trust, who they know understand them, and who they can call their own. A Chinese person employed by a Western company in a liaison capacity is in a position to understand the difficulties facing both parties. The Chinese may use this person as their consultant as well as ask for his or her opinions and advice.

A good strategy for a Western enterprise is to use a Chinese person as an unofficial communication line. This allows the parties involved to talk things over privately and establish a common ground. If the Chinese feel they cannot participate in the business proposal of a particular Western company, they can communicate it through this unofficial line of communication without it appearing on official records. This removes the possible risk of embarrassment, allows the Chinese to save face, and lessens the factor of fear present in Chinese political, social, and economic affairs. The use of a Chinese person as an unofficial line of communication allows the parties to test the water without worrying about possible future liabilities.

The Chinese have fierce internal conflicts. Western companies should consider the positions of all people involved in a desired venture, including their Chinese partners. By using the unofficial communicator to eliminate obvious difficulties, it is possible to create a less threatening and more harmonious working environment. The Chinese will willingly choose the company able to create such an environment as a business partner.

Individual Profit Center

An understanding of individual profit centers requires a knowledge of Chinese society and individual characteristics. For example, in some cases, the good of all is less important to a Chinese person than individual good. In communist or socialist societies, profit centers are not necessarily limited to cash. They can be many other things as well. A knowledge of how each person functions is necessary to determine individual profit centers. Once profit centers have been identified, a company can present itself in an attractive light; almost as if one is creating a bait for the Chinese to grab.

Face

A common characteristic which can be used to the benefit of the Westerner is the concept of face to the Chinese. Face is often related to status, so anything you can do for the Chinese which imparts status gives them face and can reduce obstacles to business transactions. Making use of this can give a company an extra competitive edge.

Bait

An understanding of the Chinese "mooching" characteristic can also turn the tables to the Westerner's advantage, by allowing the Westerner to tantalize his Chinese partners with an alluring bait.

Enhancing Your Chinese Partner's Position

The Chinese often use the Western businessman as leverage to accomplish goals which may be mutually beneficial. For instance, a Chinese businessman may want his Western partner to sell a proposed project to department heads or top Chinese officials. The Chinese tend to believe foreign businessmen over their own staff and put greater weight on the foreign expert's suggestions and projections. As an authority in a particular field, a Western businessman may be able to enhance his Chinese partner's position, and should readily do so if the opportunity presents itself. Interdepartmental communication or communication between a subordinate and his superior is often less effective than the information conveyed directly from a foreign specialist.

Lessen or Add to the Burden of Fear

The Chinese businessman will appreciate it whenever his foreign partners can assist in lessening the fear factor, which can help the Western businessman gain much ground. Fear is always present when Chinese present a project and ask a superior for approval and support because if something goes wrong they are marked for life. A portion of the weight of responsibility is lifted from the Chinese partner if the Western businessman is able to directly participate by taking on some of the financial or technical responsibility to ensure the success of the project. It is especially true that if the foreign company has a good reputation internationally, the path for joint cooperation of two parties can be smoothed.

However, in exchange for lessening the burden of fear for their Chinese partners, the Western company places its professional credibility on the line. So, be aware of the level of integrity of your Chinese partners. When a Western company takes on most of the burden to ensure the success of a venture, it is very necessary for them to create incentives for the Chinese to perform their end of bargain. I believe that too much fear will prevent the parties of a project from ever reaching a workable agreement. But, if there is no fear at all, there will be no incentive to complete the agreement. A certain amount of fear in a project involving the Chinese is healthy and will help ensure its completion. I personally do not like those joint ventures wherein the Western company brings working capital, equipment, and technology, and the Chinese provide manpower and a location. In these ventures, the Chinese have everything to gain and nothing to lose.

The factor of fear to the Chinese also contributes to their preference for large companies as working partners. The Chinese feel a larger company is more secure and is, therefore, able to afford to lose some money. They feel this will cause less trouble for the Chinese in the future.

Japanese Versus Chinese Protocol

For those who have had much experience in dealing with Japanese businessmen, your Japanese business manner (learned by the Westerner with such difficulty), if transferred to the Chinese business world, will become a liability.

You will find the Chinese to be much less formal, easier to talk to, and more accessible than their Japanese counterparts. This openness is especially visible among the Northern Chinese.

Japanese business dealings and negotiations are more formal and rigid affairs, full of exacting protocol requirements. This reflects the more rigid social formalities which exist in Japanese society. The Japanese expect that Westerners will follow these rules. In the opinion of the Chinese, the Japanese are too stuffy and nit-picking.

American openness is well received by the Chinese. Chinese protocol is comparatively informal. They are usually willing to forgive Westerners in the event of a mistake in etiquette. However, the essential rules necessary in dealing with the Chinese are hidden from foreign eyes and are not accessible at the surface level. They exist as unwritten rules in the Chinese mind.

A Japanese businessman told me one time that "doing business with the people in Taiwan is just like doing business with the Japanese." This is because Taiwan has been controlled by Japan for fifty years. Taiwanese understand the Japanese mentality and are therefore good judges of the two business cultures.

Taiwanese businessmen are very effective when dealing with the Japanese. I have discussed the differences in doing business with the Chinese and Japanese with many of these people. They have expressed that, when working with the Chinese, it is easier to reach an agreement but harder to enforce the agreement's integrity. This is because of the slippery and more self-centered nature of the Chinese. On the other hand, it is harder to reach an agreement when working with the Japanese, but once you have reached it, it is solid. Unless you do something to really goof it up, your project will reach its intended end.

Allow Them to Show Off Their Swordsmanship

The Chinese government has relaxed its attitude toward freedom of creativity. They have recognized the importance of allowing the able individual to contribute his creativity. This is essential to the success of China's modernization.

The Chinese government has started to look at things more realistically since opening its doors to West. A recent study reported to the central government that the average Chinese individual does only three hours of productive work per day, and that the country's use of machines is less than fifty percent of capacity.

However, the April 25, 1988 edition of the People's Daily (overseas Chinese edition) showed a cartoon in which a large government enterprise advertised for employees by waving flags which said, "High Pay," "Excellent Benefits," and "Bonuses" but everyone flew past their stand and rushed to a small company which had only one statement on their banner. This was, "We offer you a chance to show off your swordsmanship" which in modern terms means, "We will allow you to contribute and be creative."

Most Chinese people grow up with the the desire to be hard working and are excellent at their creative expression. However under the political systems of the past there has been a lack of incentive for individual commitment. This placed the Chinese individual in a position where he was better off if he avoided any commitment to excellence. However, if the Western company can secure control of the project, by allowing and encouraging a commitment to excellence on the part of the work force, a surge of individual creativity will be the result.

Beware of Middle Management and Party Members

According to the World Journal (Chinese Language Edition), the president of Xian Film Studio, Mr. Wu Tian Ming, said during an interview, "One of the biggest barriers and obstacles to the industrialization and modernization process in China are those of the extreme left who make up a portion of middle management and are party members. Although Chairman Mao is gone, there exist still in China many who follow his way of thinking, especially in middle management." During my business dealings in China, I have been told many times to beware of middle management people. The Chinese advise me to do business directly, to go straight to the top. I have found that, if you get stuck negotiating with middle management, you will run into a host of difficulties. These people like to justify their existence. They like to show they have power, that they can make things happen. As a result, they cause many times more trouble than would have come about had they been bypassed all together. So, avoid them.

Time is Time, Money is Money

In the West, we say, "Time is money." In the Socialist-Communist society, this concept is practically nonexistent. Even though China has opened herself up to Western business, the idea that time is money is one that is very slow to take hold. Recently The World Journal published an interview with Shuen Xiao Lieng, a Chinese-American filmmaker who recently completed filming in China. She said a film which takes three months to film in the United States will take over a year in China. To the Chinese, time is unlimited. Plastic film, however, has to be bought and is very expensive. So, they rehearsed every shot over and over until it was, although perfect, no longer spontaneous. There was no room to edit or change anything after the filming because there was only one shot of every scene.

Top Down and Bottom Up

If I wish to do business with General Motors, Nike, Intel or any other large US corporation, the higher in the management team I can align myself, the better will be my success rate. In China, this is only half the story. You must strive to get the best terms at the negotiating table with the high officials by utilizing all of your know-how, including gaining their trust and friendship. This is called "Top Down."

But to ensure the success of your project, your second action should be "Bottom Up." You must quickly gain the cooperation of lower level workers and management, so they will take your project to heart. This process plays a vital role in the success of your venture because the willingness to cooperate at a lower level cannot be controlled by upper management.

Since, the Chinese do not wish to make unnecessary enemies among themselves, often job integrity is left by the wayside. They don't like to fire people, even when necessary. The government promotes efficient operation. The government can sing all the tunes they want to the world, but day-to-day reality is a different thing. A Chinese cartoon appeared recently that showed a Lost and Found department with a large lock on the unclaimed goods. In with the unclaimed goods was a huge book, entitled "Professional Integrity." No one had claimed it. So, you are wise to practice "Top Down and Bottom Up," along with the creation of good incentive programs, to ensure the success of your project.

Honesty - With Caution

The Chinese have a saying, "If you don't fight, you will never get close." So, do not be afraid of confrontation if you are guided carefully by an individual well versed in Chinese society. An honest confrontation can result in a great deal of ground gained and can create a better understanding of each other's difficulties. The method of execution is of vital importance. And you must never forget you are a foreigner. Know your assets and liabilities. An honest, open confrontation is more suitable when dealing with the Northern Chinese, and less effective with the Chinese of the South.

Western companies should not too readily or too honestly share their difficulties with the Chinese. Too much or misplaced honesty can create confusion and may be interpreted as incompetence. The Chinese people have a limited understanding of Western business practices and political structures. When the Western business man says he is unable to accomplish something, his statements may be misconstrued to mean he is not good enough. If there is a problem and it must be explained, it is best to go into a great deal of detail and explain the whole system. Negative information should not be given in a narrow sense, but should be explained as part of the entire picture. The Chinese appreciate this kind of sincerity and willingness to educate them.

Appeal to the Chinese Inner Culture

To some Chinese, the accomplishment of a goal is more satisfying if done elaborately. The Chinese want to look important and prestigious, which is not always practical. For example, China does not yet have a stable electrical supply, but some Chinese officials may want a state-of-the-art computer system to track production at a facility where a manual system would do very nicely. Low-tech mechanical controls would be more reliable than electronic control and would eliminate possible future problems resulting from the unstable supply of electricity. But, practicality often is considered less important than symbols of prestige. When confronted with this type of problem, it is best to tactfully lead the Chinese officials toward the most efficient and practical solution, while making this solution as elaborate as possible.

There are two large U.S. soft drink companies in China. The leading company in the U.S., Coca Cola Co., is also taking the greater portion of the Chinese market. The reason it does so well in China is because it is the Number One soft drink company in the world and is, to the Chinese, more elite and prestigious. Why do the Chinese drink soft drinks from the U.S.? The Chinese have their own carbonated soft drinks. Why choose Coke? Why even try it? It is much more expensive. The Chinese drink Coke as a status symbol. It is a symbol of success. The rich Chinese drink Coke; the poor Chinese drink tea.

The most popular book in China today is not Mao's, nor is it a book on Marxism. The most popular book in China today is the autobiography of Lee Iacocca. The Chinese want to learn how they can get ahead. When a Chinese is successful, he can have things and privileges nobody else has. To consume a product which is the best known of its kind in the world is a great privilege because of its expense, and is very prestigious.

Coca Cola Co. has another advantage in the Chinese market. It has a wonderful name! And remember that China is a country where the choosing of the right name is very important. Translated literally into Chinese, Coca Cola means "Delight to the Mouth and Delight to the Heart."

It will be difficult for Pepsi Cola to top Coke's sales in China. Pepsi Cola cannot make its product more desirable to the Chinese by lowering its price. The price needs to stay up to maintain its image as a status symbol. They need something extra to bait the consumer. The distributors need to aggressively promote their product.

Sales could be enhanced by embarking on a nationwide campaign to create a "dream come true." There are two dreams shared by most Chinese. One is a trip abroad, the other is a scholarship for study in a foreign country for their children. The Chinese love to travel because they have been so sheltered for the past 40 years. And the education of children always has the highest priority in

Chinese society. Even when an individual has much money, these two dreams are hard to realize. There are tight currency controls and few contacts with foreign individuals. An enticing promotion would be a contest resulting in the winning of a trip to the United States or a scholarship to a U.S. school.

During 1987, I saw a Chinese cartoon about three foreign competitors who come to China with contracts and products. It showed the Chinese ignoring the two companies with the best products and the finest service and choosing the one that offered them a free trip to America. The Chinese fascination with travel has led to many trips for observation and study to the U.S. and Europe at government expense.

Pepsi Cola should have explored the practical nature of the Chinese people since it cannot outstrip Coca Cola in the race for prestige. There are infinite possibilities in the Chinese market. Every hint, gesture or speech can give clues how to best take advantage of the situation. One interesting point is that I have asked many Chinese about the taste of the two colas and have discovered that most prefer the taste of Pepsi Cola.

I telephoned Pepsi Cola's offices in New York state and asked them about their marketing strategies in China. The answer I received was that they have no marketing strategies in China. They just make their product available.

American, Japanese, European and Hong Kong Business Tactics

Happy, open, direct personalities have become the trademark of American business people. These American qualities are valued highly over those of other nationalities. But when it comes to understanding the subtleties of the Chinese mind, American business people and politicians usually take a back seat to Europeans and other Asians.

The Japanese, perhaps more than any other cultural group on Earth, have the greatest understanding of the Chinese mind. This understanding allows the Japanese to create compelling bait. Despite feelings of resentment towards the Japanese, stemming from Japan's ambitious military history with China and present economic invasion, the Chinese are hooked again and again by the Japanese. The Chinese know this, but as the Japanese know to make their products inexpensive and irresistible, the Chinese cannot resist.

Many Europeans have become very competitive in the Chinese market, even to the degree of becoming a threat to Japanese companies. Some large deals have been lost by the Japanese to European competitors. There are European countries who have offered loans to China with the stipulation that the loan proceeds can only be used to purchase goods from the lending country. These loans are generally made at low interest rates and have long terms. The Chinese know when they buy goods from that country the prices may be higher than they would have to pay elsewhere. But, the long-term, low-interest loans are very inviting. Also, the decision makers in China are of the older generation. They know the price today may be high, but they consider having the product or machine immediately with only a small monthly payment as an advantage. The current decision makers feel it is not their problem to worry about the person who will eventually have the responsibility of full repayment of the loan. Europeans have successfully taken a share of the Chinese market from the Japanese using this method.

The Hong Kong Chinese have a natural advantage in dealing with China. Some of the practices engaged in by the Chinese of Hong Kong may not be suitable for the Westerner to attempt, but the Westerner should be aware of them nonetheless. For instance, expensive gifts are often given by Hong Kong business people to their Chinese partners. These gifts are such things as refrigerators, televisions, electronic consumer items or scholarships for their children to schools in the United States or Europe. Although these are bribes, the Hong Kong Chinese are able to present them in such an elegant manner that the bribery is disguised. These gentle bribes sweeten proposed financial deals.

The Power From Within

After you have carefully read this book and perhaps memorized the "36 Strategies," there is one more most important element, without which you won't be able to freely recognize the Chinese mind games and their strategies. The element which will allow you to recognize and utilize the "Art of War" and the "36 Strategies" and which develops the needed sensitivity to the Asian culture lies within the space of the "Inner Silence."

The power of "Inner Silence" is the root of all creativity, all understanding, all intuition; it can reveal every motivation and the intention of your Asian counterpart. When in doubt, center yourself, dive deep into the familiar place of that Inner Silence, where the answers have always existed. All knowledge can be useful and of benefit to mankind because of that which is within your own Inner Silence.

> Lao Tzu said:
>> Something existed
>> Before the creation of Heaven and Earth.
>> In the silence and the void,
>> Ever alone and changeless,
>> She prevails all.
>> Conceive Her as the mother of the universe.
>> I know not Her name,
>> And call Her - Tao.

A Foreigner should use the information he gathers about China. Experience it. Absorb and digest it. Make it your own. The Chinese believe that to learn one thing allows one to know three more things. One principle leads to many more things using the same principle. This is the way one should learn. Learn one thing, but know much more by experiencing the essence.

An understanding of the Chinese mind is crucial when dealing in China. But no less important are honesty, sincerity, and a willingness to participate with the Chinese people. A high level of integrity and knowledge are needed to prevent being trapped by the Chinese games. The games must be understood and transcended. The greater the understanding one has of the Chinese mind games, the greater the odds of success in dealings with the Chinese.

APPENDIX:

THE COMMON BACKGROUND SHARED BY ALL THE CHINESE PEOPLE
Creation - Mythology

Male-Female Aspect

The Mountain, Sea Scriptures, the most complete book of Chinese mythology, author unknown, is the combination of works from the Zhou dynasties, Spring-Autumn Period, Warring States and early Han.

Most popular version - Pan Gu (Male aspect) created the Universe. Nyu Wa (Female aspect) started creating Mankind from water and yellow clay. Handmade clay figures became rich people. Then, tired of the work, she dipped a rope in water and yellow clay and dripped the resulting mud unto the Earth, infusing it with life, to create poor people.

2nd creation version - Huai Nan Zi God of Yin and God of Yang created Heaven and Earth. Established Yin and Yang and eight directions. The Yang God is in charge of Heaven and above, the Yin God is in charge of the Earth and below.

Gods & Humans

Nyu Wa - The first match maker. Gave humans the ability to reproduce themselves because She was tired of all the work involved in making them.

There was war between the God of Fire and the God of Water - Good (light) vs. Evil (darkness). They fought from Heaven to Earth. The Water God had two sons; one good, one bad. The bad son joined the war with two other helpers. During the war, Heaven's pillars were destroyed. The good son loved to travel so did nothing but travel. He was traveling during the war. After his death, people called him Zhu San. In the ancient times, when one wanted to travel, he or she first had to worship Zhu San by giving a banquet in order to earn God's grace and protection.

Ancient Chinese prople believed the reason Heaven is above is because there are four large pillars holding it up. The mother of Earth, Nyu Wa, at one time had to repair the sky and Earth. However, due to some imperfection in the repair work, Eastern China was made lower than Western China. There were holes in the Eastern part of China which caused all the rivers to travel eastward to the Pacific Ocean, the Earth's largest hole.

After her death, Nyu Wa entered the Ninth Heaven and gave glory to nature.

The Origin of The Chinese: Children of Yan Di and Huang Di

Yan Di - Sun God

Taught plantation, agriculture, and medical science. Also called the Agriculture God. The sun is the source of agriculture and good health.

Huang Di

Invented Compass (2000 BC)
Wife Leizhu originated Sericulture and silk-weaving techniques.

Huang Di gave the job of "God of Gods" to his grandson. He stayed on Earth. Intermarriage of the children of Huang Di and Yan Di gave birth to the Chinese people.

Sky Ladder - The Passage to Heaven.

People used to be able to go to Heaven by way of the "Sky Ladder." Because so many wars were fought between Heaven and Earth, the Jade Emperor ordered the removal of the sky ladder to keep the Gods and humans apart, Yin and Yang in order, and keep peace between Heaven and Earth.

Brief Outline of Chinese History

B.C.

360,000

Men of primitive species called Sinanthropus Pekinensis established themselves in the lower Yellow River valley.

2697 **Huang Di:**
Huang Di. (ruled 100 years)

2597
Huang Di's son (ruled 84 years)

2513
Grandson (ruled 78 years)

2435
Great grandson (ruled 70 years)

2357 **Tang Dynasty:**
Yao (ruled 100 years) (died 2258 B.C.)

2255 **Yu Dynasty:**
Suen (ruled 48 years) (died 2208 B.C.)

2205 **Hsia Dynasty:**
440 years, 17 generations.

1766   **Shang Dynasty:**
644 years, 28 generations. Flourished in the Yellow River valley. Feudalism.

1122   **Zou Dynasty:**
352 years, 12 generations. Consolidated and extended the central power to the Yangtze valley. Strong unity, centralization, feudalism.

770   **East Zou Dynasty:**
515 years, 22 generations. Weak unity, decentralization and total division in the warring states. Feudalism. Rise of philosophic schools, Confucius, Taoism (Lau Tsu, Zhung Tsu), Han Fei Tzu.

770   **Spring-Autumn period**

476   **Warring States:**
Seven strong rulers.

221   **Chin Dynasty:**
15 years, 3 emperors. Strong unity and centralization. Great wall built, the First Emperor, who unites China. His successor is murdered after a three-year reign.

202
Chou, Han fighting. (Xiang Yu and Liu Bang)

206   **Han Dynasty: 212 years, 13 emperors.**
Liu Pang, founder of Han Dynasty. Centralization, unity, establishment of bureaucracy.

140-87
The Emperor Wu Di extends Chinese power into Western Asia, Korea, Southeast Asia. Confucianism and Taoism become a state cult. Wu Di was a devotee of the (distorted) Taoist superstitions.

A.D.

9-23

Wang Mang, a nephew of the Empress, usurped the throne and attempted to redistribute land to the peasants.

25 East Han Dynasty:
195 years, 12 emperors. Han Dynasty is restored. Its forces reached Vietnam and Afghanistan.

65

Buddhism entered China. Emperor Ming Di sent scholar to Central Asia.

68

Built Buddhist temples.

220 Three Kingdoms:
59 years, China divided into three kingdoms. The beginning of the decline of Northwest China and growth of Southeast China.

265 Jien Dynasty:
52 years, 4 emperors. Weak unity.

317 East Jien Dynasty:
103 years, 11 emperors. There were also five barbarian states, six countries, four Southern Dynasties, and five Northern Dynasties. Buddhism flourished.

581 Sui Dynasty:
38 years, 3 emperors. Sui emperors again consolidated China, rebuilt the Great Wall and employed five million people in construction of an elaborate water transport system (a handmade canal from Northern China to Southern China) for the Emperor's travel pleasure.

618 Tang Dynasty:

289 years, 20 emperors. Li Yuan and his son Li Shiming founded the Tang Dynasty. Golden Age of art and literature. Government and Civil Service examination system perfected.

629-645

Chinese monk went to India for scriptures. Japan sent scholars.

635

Islam entered China.

690-705

Empress Wou established Zhou Dynasty.

755

Rebellion of An Lu-San.

907

Five Dynasties and Ten States. China divided. Widespread use of paper money.

960 North Sung Dynasty:

167 years, 9 emperors. Division.

1127 South Sung Dynasty:

Jien captured two emperors. Capitol transferred to Nanjing. Chu Tzu's teaching flourish.

1271-1292

Marco Polo makes his historic journey to China and Southeast Asia.

1279 Yuan Dynasty:

93 years, 9 emperors. Mongols destroyed Jien, Sung, Liou, Xia and completed the conquest of China;

1281

4,400 ships and 140,000 soldiers totally destroyed in a invasion of Japan.

1282
Mongols killed Prime Minister of Sung, Wen Tian Xiang.

1368 **Ming Dynasty:**
276 years, 16 emperors. The Mongols were driven out of China.

1405-1433
Ming emperors sent huge sea expedition as far as Africa.

1514-1600
Western traders attempted to establish trade relations. Europeans came by sea.

1582-1610
Father Matteo Ricci, a Jesuit, established the first Roman Catholic mission in China.

1644 **Ching Dynasty:**
367 years, 10 emperors. Manchus conquered China.

1793
Lord Macartney tried unsuccessfully to establish British trade relations with China.

1796-1835
Emperor Ren Zong (Chia Ching) prohibited importing of opium, but the traffic increased to 19,000 chests annually.

1839
Commissioner Lin Zhe Xu (Hsu) was assigned to Canton and forced the English to surrender $11million worth of opium. The Opium War between China and English began.

1842

The Opium War was settled by the treaty of Nanjing. Five ports were forced open for trading. Hong Kong was ceded to Britain. Western powers received legal jurisdiction over their own nationals in China. China paid 21 million ounces of silver for damages.

1853-1864

The Tai Ping rebels captured Nanjing and held it as their capital.

1858

Britain and France forced the signing of the Treaty of Tienjin by which China granted still further concessions.

1894-1895

Sino-Japanese War culminated in the Treaty of Shimonoseki, under which extensive concessions were granted to Japan.

1894

Sue Yat-sen lead an abortive revolt against the Manchus.

1898

Emperor Kuang Xu (Hsu) tried unsuccessfully to modernize China during "100 Days" of reform. Rebellions became widespread. Anti-foreign and anti-Christian agitation increased.

1900-1901

Foreign legations in Bejing were seized during the Boxer Uprising. In retaliation, foreign nations forced the payment of immense indemnities.

1911 **Republic of China**

Successful revolution brought the overthrow of the Ching Dynasty. Sun Yat-sen was chosen first President but was forced out by the Northern warlordS.

1921

The Chinese Communist Party was organized at a congress held in Shanghai.

1924

After promises of Russian aid, Sun's party, the Kuomintang, allowed Communists to become members. Chiang Kai-shek was named head of the Whampoa Military Academy.

1925

March 12, 9:30 am, Dr. Sun Yat-sen, father of the founder of the Republic of China, died.

1926-1928

Chiang Kai-shek launched an expedition against the Northern warlords and eventually broke their power.

1927

Chiang crushed the Communists in Shanghai.

1934-35

After attacks by the Nationalists, Mao Zedong led his followers northward on the Long March.

1937

On July 7th, Japan invaded China. Nationalists and Communists formed a united front to fight the Japanese.

1945-1947

At U.S. urging, Mao and Chiang conferred on the formation of a coalition government.

1949 The People's Republic of China

The Communists captured Beijing. On October 1, Mao established the People's Republic of China.

1947-1952

The Communists began land reform. Opponents, or suspected opponents, of the regime were executed or sent to labor camps. The Korean War began. Chinese "Volunteers" crossed the Yalu to fight U.N. troops.

1955

Mao Zedong ordered collectivization of farms.

1958

Mao initiated the "Great Leap Forward" program and reorganized the country into communes. Reports of gains from the program were exaggerated.

1963

Disputes between China and the Soviet Union over the appropriate road to achieve Communism broke into the open.

History of China's Population Change

A.D. Year		Total Population
2	(Western Han Dynasty)	59,590,000
755	(Tang Dynasty)	52,910,000
1080	(Song Dynasty)	33,300,000
1578	(Ming Dynasty)	60,960,000
1741	(Ching Dynasty)	143,410,000
1840	(Ching Dynasty)	412,000,000
1911	(Republic of China)	405,810,000
1949	(Founding of PRC)	541,670,000
1982	(July 1st)	1,031,882,511

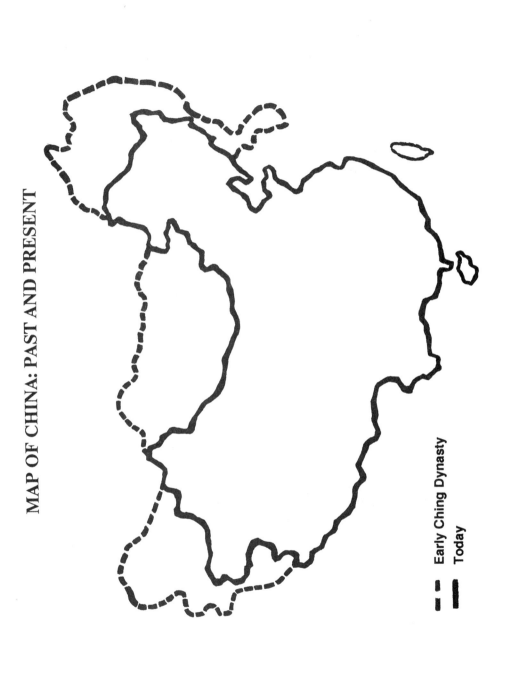

MAP OF CHINA: PAST AND PRESENT

Early Ching Dynasty
Today

INDEX

REQUEST FOR PROFESSIONAL CONSULTATION

TO ASIAN MARKETING CONSULTANTS, INC.

Attention: Chin-ning Chu

P.O. Box 1420-C

Beaverton, Oregon 97075-1420

FAX: 503-641-3227

Telex: 5101006290 SHARED SEC SVC

Please contact me to arrange a telephone consultation. Enclosed is $75.00 which is the fee for one-half hour's consultation. I understand I will billed for any time exceeding one half hour plus telephone charges.

Name: _____

Company: _____

Position: _____

Address: _____

_____

City, State, Zip: _____

Phone: _____

Best Time to Call: _____

FAX Number: _____

Telex Number: _____

Consultation Fee: $150 per hour ($75.00 minimum, one-half hour)

Signature: _____

REQUEST FOR PROFESSIONAL
CONSULTATION

TO ASIAN MARKETING CONSULTANTS, INC.
Attention: Chin-ning Chu
P.O. Box 1420-C
Beaverton, Oregon 97075-1420
FAX: 503-641-3227
Telex: 5101006290 SHARED SEC SVC

Please contact me to arrange a telephone consultation. Enclosed is $75.00 which is the fee for one-half hour's consultation. I understand I will billed for any time exceeding one half hour plus telephone charges.

Name: _____

Company: _____

Position: _____

Address: _____

_____

City, State, Zip:_____

Phone: _____

Best Time to Call: _____

FAX Number: _____

Telex Number: _____

Consultation Fee: $150 per hour ($75.00 minimum, one-half hour)

Signature: _____

ORDER FORM

AMC Publishing, Inc.
Post Office Box 1420E
Beaverton, Oregon 97075-1420 U.S.A
Telephone (503) 644-2438

Please send me the following:

The Chinese Mind Game **$19.95**
Traveling in China: The Real Story .... **$ 9.95**
Learning Chinese the Natural Way for Business and Professional People **$85.00**

(An 8 hour Audio Cassette Language Course. This new approach, using simple, real-life situations - the way the Chinese children learn to speak their native tongue. It culminates with a lesson on how to deliver a basic speech at a banquet or meeting in Chinese.)

Name: (Please print) _____

Company: _____

Address: _____

Phone ( ) _____

Shipping: $3 for the first book and $2 for each additional book.   Audio Language Course, $4 for each set.

Check enclosed for $ _____   (Make check payable to AMC Publishing, Inc.)

Chin-ning Chu is available for Keynote speaking, training and seminars on the subjects related to marketing in the Pacific Rim.

ORDER FORM

AMC Publishing, Inc.
Post Office Box 1420E
Beaverton, Oregon 97075-1420 U.S.A
Telephone (503) 644-2438

Please send me the following:

The Chinese Mind Game **$19.95**
Traveling in China: The Real Story ....**$ 9.95**
Learning Chinese the Natural Way for Business and Professional People **$85.00**

(An 8 hour Audio Cassette Language Course. This new approach, using simple, real-life situations - the way the Chinese children learn to speak their native tongue. It culminates with a lesson on how to deliver a basic speech at a banquet or meeting in Chinese.)

Name: (Please print) _____

Company: _____

Address: _____

Phone ( ) _____

Shipping: $3 for the first book and $2 for each additional book. Audio Language Course, $4 for each set.

Check enclosed for $ _____ (Make check payable to AMC Publishing, Inc.)

Chin-ning Chu is available for Keynote speaking, training and seminars on the subjects related to marketing in the Pacific Rim.

Notes

Notes

Notes

Notes